# Birthplace
# of
# Montana

# A History of Fort Benton

## By John G. Lepley

Library of Congress Number 99-75253
ISBN 1-57510-068-1

Published for John G. Lepley by:
Pictorial Histories Publishing Company
713 South Third Street West, Missoula, Montana 59801
phpc @ montana . com

Cover Painting and Line Drawings by David Parchen

# Dedication

## To Joel F. Overholser

Fort Benton's gifted historian from whom I gained much of my knowledge and enthusiasm.

# Introduction

From its establishment in 1846 until the turn-of-the-century, Fort Benton's primacy in the history of the northern plains is unequaled. Called the "Birthplace of Montana," Fort Benton is the oldest continuously occupied white settlement in Montana.

The Missouri River was the waterway into the northern plains, to points farther west and north into Canada. The river created Fort Benton, and their histories merge into a single fascinating story of Western folklore.

The rich and famous, scoundrels and killers, merchants and gamblers rubbed elbows on Front Street and the levee as they arrived and embarked aboard mackinaws, keelboats and steamboats. Three-fourths of all freight that came into the region was unloaded on Fort Benton's levee and transported to all points of the compass. Until the coming of the railroad, Fort Benton was the "Chicago of the Plains."

In 1965 Fort Benton was designated a National Historic Landmark; the Upper Missouri became part of the National Wild and Scenic River System in 1975. The significant role they played in settlement of the American and Canadian West accorded them national and international importance in the history of both nations.

# Contents

*"The Best towns in Montana started with whiskey and hitchin' racks,
It's a cinch it wasn't Coca Cola and Garages."*
C. M. Russell

# FORT BENTON, MONTANA

## National Historic Landmark

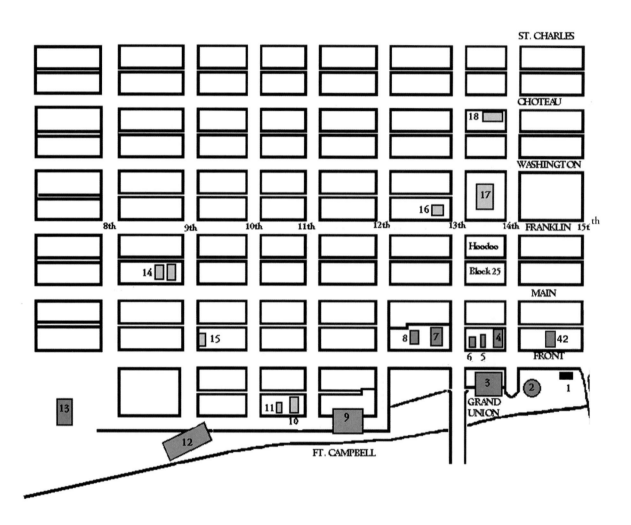

ST. CHARLES

CHOTEAU

WASHINGTON

18

17

16

8th  9th  10th  11th  12th  13th  14th  FRANKLIN  15t^th

Hoodoo

Block 25

MAIN

14

15

8  7

4  42

6  5  FRONT

11

10

13

3

2  1

GRAND
UNION

9

12

FT. CAMPBELL

## Major Sites

A. Old Fort Benton
B. Montana Agricultural Center
   Hornaday Buffalo and Gallery
   Montana's Museum of Agriculture
   1920's Homestead Village
C. Museum of the Upper Missouri

1. Old Engine House
   and Information Center
2. Shep Memorial and
   Shepherd's Court
3. Grand Union Hotel
4. Stockmen's National Bank
5. Bank of Northern Montana
6. Gans and Klein Clothing

7. Murphy Neel and Co.
8. Davidson and Moffitt Saddlery
   (River Press)
9. Site of Fort Campbell
10. Coulson Steamboat Offices
11. Major Guido Ilges Home
12. Site of Fort LaBarge
13. Site of Montana's first municipal
    water and electric plant

# BIRTHPLACE OF MONTANA

## Chicago of the Plains

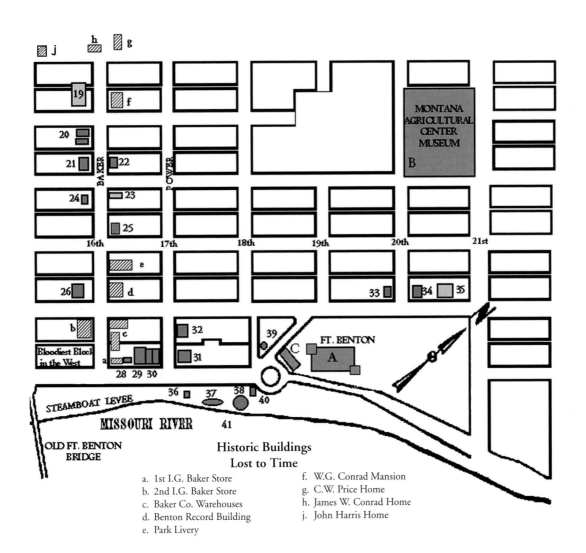

MONTANA AGRICULTURAL CENTER MUSEUM

FT. BENTON

Bloodiest Block in the West

STEAMBOAT LEVEE

MISSOURI RIVER 41

OLD FT. BENTON BRIDGE

### Historic Buildings
### Lost to Time

a. 1st I.G. Baker Store
b. 2nd I.G. Baker Store
c. Baker Co. Warehouses
d. Benton Record Building
e. Park Livery

f. W.G. Conrad Mansion
g. C.W. Price Home
h. James W. Conrad Home
j. John Harris Home

14. Homes of the Admirals
15. Harber Home
16. Rufus Payne Home
17. Chouteau County Courthouse
18. St. Paul's Episcopal Church
19. second Church of the Immaculate Conception
20. Baker Company Homes
21. Joseph A. Baker Home
22. Joseph H. Conrad Home

23. C.E. Conrad Wedding Bungalow
24. Blacksmith Shop
25. Methodist Church
26. Chouteau County Carnegie Library
27. Old Fort Benton Bridge
28. I.G. Baker Home
29. Chouteau House Hotel
30. T.C. Power Stores
31. T.C. Power and Bro. Mercantile
32. T.C. Power Warehouse

33. Early Home
34. George D. Patterson Home
35. D.G. Browne Home
36. Mullan Road Marker
37. Keelboat Mandan
38. State Memorial to Lewis and Clark
39. Doughboy Memorial, World War I
40. Whoop-Up Trail Marker
41. Wreck of Baby Rose (in river)
42. Masonic Temple

# Illustrations

## Maps

## Photographs

All photographs came from the Photo Archives of the
Schwinden Library or from the author's personal collection.

# Chronology

| | |
|---|---|
| 1805 | Lewis and Clark passed by site of Fort Benton on the way to the Pacific |
| 1806 | Lewis boarded the canoes at site of Fort Benton after fight with Blackfoot |
| 1807 | Manuel Lisa established the first white settlement at Fort Raymond |
| 1810 | Unsuccessful fur fort at the Three Forks of the Missouri |
| 1828 | Fort Union built on the Yellowstone River |
| 1831 | Construction of Fort Piegan at mouth of Maria's River |
| 1832 | Fort MacKenzie established in Blackfoot country |
| 1833 | Maximilian and Bodmer came to Fort MacKenzie |
| 1837 | Smallpox decimated Blackfoot |
| 1843 | Culbertson left for Fort William; Fort MacKenzie burned |
| 1844 | Fort F.A. Chardon constructed at mouth of Judith River |
| 1845 | Fort Lewis replaced Fort Chardon |
| 1846 | Border settlement at 49th parallel in Oregon |
| 1846 | Site of Fort Benton established |
| 1847 | Fort Campbell built of adobe |
| 1847 | Fort Lewis torn down and moved to Fort Benton |
| 1848 | St. Mary's Mission closed; Fort Benton only white settlement left in Montana |
| 1850 | Christmas Day Fort Benton officially named for Senator Thomas Hart Benton |
| 1850 | Fort Owen on the Bitterroot built |
| 1853 | Stevens Treaty at Fort Benton |
| 1851 | Culbertson left Fort Benton for Fort Union |
| 1855 | Blackfoot Agency at Fort Benton |
| 1855 | Steven's Treaty with the Indians |
| 1859 | Conversion to adobe completed at Fort Benton |
| 1860 | *Chippewa* and *Key West*, first steamboats at Fort Benton levee |
| 1862 | Gold discovered in Montana |
| 1862 | Building of Fort LaBarge near Fort Benton |
| 1862 | Capt. James Fisk arrived with first wagon train from Minnesota |
| 1862 | President Lincoln signed Homestead Act |
| 1863 | Carroll founded on lower river |
| 1864 | Montana Territory |
| 1865 | Blackfoot Treaty signed in Fort Benton |
| 1866 | Camp Cooke, first military post in Montana |
| 1867 | Gov. Thomas F. Meagher drowned at Fort Benton |
| 1868 | Fur fort's last year |
| 1869 | Fort Whoop-Up constructed near Lethbridge, Alberta |

| | |
|---|---|
| 1869 | Camp Cooke closed |
| 1869 | Military moved to Fort Benton |
| 1870 | Baker Massacre |
| 1870 | Second smallpox epidemic hit Blackfoot |
| 1871 | Whoop-up Trail to Canada |
| 1873 | Cypress Hills Massacre |
| 1874 | Northwest Mounted Police arrived |
| 1875 | Fort Macleod established in Alberta |
| 1876 | Custer Massacre |
| 1877 | Chief Joseph surrendered |
| 1878 | Fort Benton came of age; first brick buildings constructed |
| 1879 | Forty-nine boats arrived, biggest year |
| 1880 | Open range cattle replaced buffalo |
| 1878-1884 | Golden years of river trade |
| 1881 | Military post closed |
| 1882 | Shonkin Stock Association founded |
| 1883 | Canadian Pacific and Northern Pacific crossed the plains to the mountains |
| 1883 | Fort Benton incorporated |
| 1883 | Founding of Montana Woolgrowers Association in Fort Benton |
| 1885 | Montana Stockgrowers Association founded in Miles City |
| 1886 | Bad winter; range cattle died by the thousands |
| 1887 | Railroad arrived in Fort Benton and ended river trade |
| 1887 | Fort Benton Bridge built, first to span Missouri in Montana |
| 1888 | Fort Benton first Montana city with municipal water system and electric plant |
| 1889 | Montana Statehood |
| 1890 | T.C. Power elected to the U.S. Senate |
| 1890 | Last commercial boat arrived, *F.Y. Batchelor* |
| 1906 | C.N. Pray elected to U.S. House of Representatives |
| 1907 | End of the open range |
| 1908 | Extended Homestead Act opened up Montana |
| 1908 | Arrival of homesteaders in Montana |
| 1908-1917 | Homestead Era |
| 1917-1921 | Drought and despair; farm people left Montana by the thousands |
| 1921 | *Mandan's* last trip to Fort Benton |
| 1921 | Dedication of Doughboy Statue |
| 1928 | Chouteau County Montana's leading wheat producer |
| 1929-1939 | Depression |
| 1937 | Boat Race; last boats upriver from St. Louis |
| 1939-1945 | World War II |
| 1946 | Fort Benton's Centennial |
| 1958 | Dedication of Museum of the Upper Missouri |
| 1976 | U.S. Bicentennial |
| 1976 | Dedication of Montana's State Memorial to Lewis and Clark |

*Chapter 1*

# The River West

*There were many routes West, but the most luxurious and expeditious was by steamboat up the Missouri from St. Louis to the Head of Navigation in the foothills of the Rockies at Fort Benton.*

## Northern Passage

The mighty Missouri provided pioneers with one of the three main routes to the west. The Santa Fe and Oregon Trails were long, slow land passages into the American frontier; the Missouri provided a much quicker waterway deep into the Rockies. From St. Louis travelers reached northwestern United States and Canada by boat. They journeyed over 2000 miles upriver in little more than a month to the head of navigation at Fort Benton. From the opening of the Northwest, the Missouri River and Fort Benton histories were so interwoven that it is impossible to separate them. This is the story of the river and its innermost port.

## The Upper Missouri

The upper river begins at today's Montana-North Dakota border where the Yellowstone, the Missouri's largest tributary, flows into the Missouri. The Missouri then flows south and eastward to join the Mississippi at St. Louis. The stretch of the river above Fort Union presented a barrier as formidable to river transportation as the Blackfoot.

In 1822 Fort Floyd, later called Fort Union, was built by William Ashley at the mouth of the Yellowstone. For quite some time it was the farthest upriver post on the edge of the high plains. Gradual penetration of the corridor continued for twenty-five years until some permanency was gained through construction of Fort Benton in 1846.

*Below: The White Cliffs of the Missouri inspire beauty and awe. Early travelers commented in their journals of this most special place.*

1

# Three Main Routes to the American West

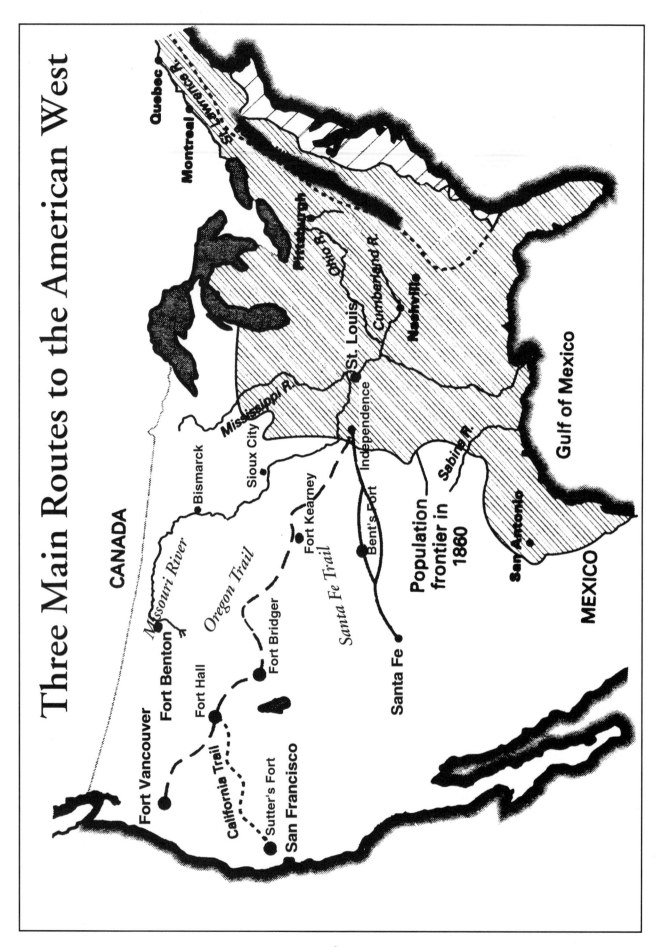

## Fort Union to Cow Island

Parties ventured periodically into the region at the mouth of the Milk River, but no enduring sites were established until after steamboats arrived on the upper river. A cluster of posts had been constructed from the mouth of the Musselshell upriver to Carroll and Rocky Point, the only sites not inundated today by the reservoir behind Fort Peck Dam.

Between Fort Union and Cow Island the river contained large bottoms. As the river annually altered its course during spring's high water, it left behind large wooded islands. Cottonwood and ash crowded one another at the river's edge. They provided protection and shade for herds of grazing animals, and later were used as fuel for the steamboats. Wood yards sprang up along the river in the 1860's when commerce to Fort Benton escalated with the discovery of gold in Montana's Rocky Mountains. The bluffs are lower in this area, cut by the river as it heads east to the Mississippi through the glacial soils of the last ice age.

At Cow Island the rocky river takes control. In low water it was difficult to cross the shelf above the island with most boats, particularly a steamboat. There were Indian crossings in the area from early times. They were used seasonally when Indians hunted in the Judith Basin then crossed back to the prairies north of the river.

## River Hazards

The series of cataracts continued upstream to Dauphin's Rapids, easily the most dangerous place on the upper river. Whether going or coming, that long stretch was a mass of hidden boulders, sand bars and rough water. All boats took care; most survived but a few were lost. One means of transport during low water was "double-tripping." A large boat unloaded at Cow Island or Dauphin's Rapids; a smaller boat

*Above left: Upriver beneath the bluff is Cow Island. At the upper end of the island is a shallow ford to cross the Missouri. The trail came down the bluff on the south side to the ford where Chief Joseph and the Nez Perce crossed in 1877.*

# Historic Upper Missouri

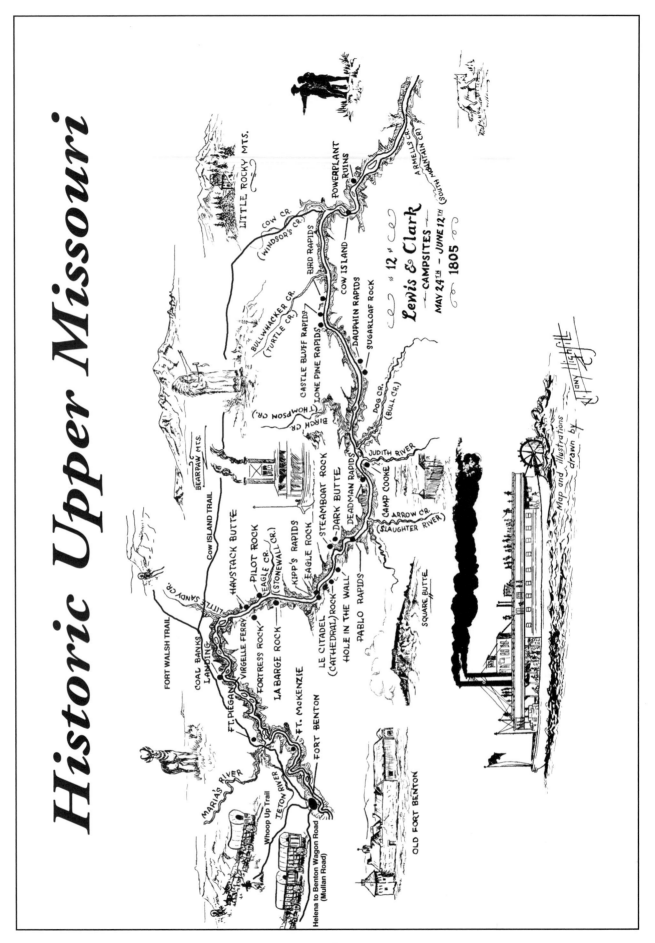

Lewis & Clark
— Campsites —
MAY 24TH – JUNE 12TH 1805

Map and illustrations drawn by

with a shallow draft continued on with its freight to Fort Benton. Many boats spent extra time negotiating this stretch of the river using spars and capstan and by off-loading.

A few miles above Dauphin's Rapids is the large open bottom where the Judith River flows in from the south. It was an ideal campsite and river crossing. Fort Chardon was built there in 1843, followed by Camp Cooke and Fort Claggett during the steamboat era. The "Mauvais Terres" end in this bottom. These badlands contain two-hundred-foot walls rising above the river, cut with deep coulees on both sides for many miles. The Mauvais Terres made passage north and south a very difficult task.

## The White Cliffs

The character of the river changes again above the Judith. After Drowned Man's Rapids, beautiful white sandstone formations break out of the hills on both sides of the river. They create tables, castles, and sentinel-like figures that rival anything in the world for beauty. Yesterday and today formations such as the

*Below: Near Grand Island the valley widens and the open bottoms and islands are covered with cottonwoods; these characterize the lower river.*

Pinnacles, Hole-in-the-Wall and the Chapel stimulate the imagination. Laced through the white sandstone are sills and dikes of Shonkinite, a granite formation radiating from the Highwood and Bears Paw Mountains. This hard granite juts out from the white sandstone to form the most prominent landmarks on the river. La Citadel, LaBarge Rock, the Grand Natural Wall and Dark Butte are massive formations of Shonkinite.

Above the mouth of the

*Above: Dauphin Rapids is the most treacherous place to navigate on the upper river. Nearby is the grave site of a party of woodhawks killed by Indians in 1865.*

*Right: The Mauvais Terres or Badlands between Cow Island and the Judith River is a high rugged canyon inhabited by Bighorn sheep.*

Judith River, creeks come into the Missouri on both sides. They rise in the island mountains that dot the prairie above the river valley. Arrow, Little Sandy and Eagle Creeks were the Indians' favorite campsites and have historical significance from the fur trade and steamboat days.

By Coal Banks Landing the white sandstone has retreated beneath the glacial till. The canyon walls are lower and the meandering Missouri resembles the river below Cow Island. Coal Banks contains exposed layers of lignite in the banks above the river. In later years the site was a low-water unloading point for the steamboats. Between Coal Banks Landing and the mouth of Maria's River is an area rich in wildlife, one of the finest for bird-watching.

## Maria's River

One of the most historic sites on the upper Missouri is

*Above: The Pinnacles or Seven Sisters is one of the most beautiful sites in the White Cliffs of the Missouri. Bodmer sketched 26 formations in this three-mile stretch of the river.*

*Left: Near Dark Butte, the Bastion is one of the many striking formations in this section of the river.*

*Left: Arrow Creek is the site of the great Gros Ventre village painted by Karl Bodmer. It is also Lewis and Clark's Slaughter River where they found many decaying bison at the river's edge.*

was constructed at the campsite. It ended tragically when the Blackfoot killed most of its inhabitants. From Ophir to Fort Benton the river encompasses the sites of Fort MacKenzie, Fort Fox-Livingston and Alexander Harvey's first trading post.

## The Crocondunez

Rowe's Landing was another low-water point. In 1859 the *Chippewa* reached Rowe's Landing before it ran out of fuel. The following year the *Chippewa* came all the way to Fort Benton and established the little river port as the head of navigation on the Missouri River, 2385 miles from St. Louis.

*Top: Hole in the Wall of the Missouri, with a beautiful collection of churches, chapels and cathedrals cut from the white sandstone behind it. To its right is a large pishkin with white bleached bones at the base of the cliff.*

Maria's River. Lewis and Clark spent more days in that single campsite than anywhere else on their western trek.

In the early 1860's Ophir, a town built to rival Fort Benton,

*Middle: The Chapel, with its hoodoo tops and arch, reminds one of castles and churches along the Rhine.*

*Right: The Valley of the Walls, a short walk from the river, is an awesome hidden canyon near the Pinnacles.*

*Top: Le Citadel, named by the voyageurs, is now a National Historic Site.*

*Left: Dark Butte is the largest granitic plug in the White Cliffs region.*

*Below: This granitic dike was called the Grand Natural Wall by Granville Stuart on his trip in 1880.*

Below the entrance of Shonkin Creek into the Missouri is the Crocondunez. There the Teton River and the Missouri are separated by a narrow neck of land. Across the top of the Crocondunez was a trail used by Indians as they traveled from their camps on the Teton to Fort Benton.

The Teton is several feet higher than the Missouri. Water flows underground and bubbles out on the Missouri side forming a spring. Since the time of Lewis

*Right: Steamboat Rock high on a hill away from the river and near Dark Butte*

*Far right: LaBarge Rock was named for steamboat Captain Joseph LaBarge of St. Louis.*

and Clark, it has been called Grog Springs. While camped there, Lewis became deathly ill, and treated himself with a bitter potion of boiled chokecherry bark and the next day was able to continue upstream.

## Journey's End

Signal Point comes into view above Shonkin Creek. From that vantage point young boys watched for steamboats, then signaled to the townspeople "steamboat 'round the bend!" The north side of the river opens into a large bottom; at one

*Right: Eye of the Needle (top right) across from Eagle Creek, now lost forever due to vandals.*

*Right: Eagle Creek in the White Cliffs was called Stonewall Creek by Lewis and Clark and was their campsite on May 31, 1805.*

*Left:* Coal Banks Landing was a low water port and served Fort Assiniboine during the 1880's. Steamboat Peninah is unloading for the bull trains headed north.

time there were three forts in that area, including Fort Benton.

During twenty-five years of steamboating, Fort Benton's levee stretched a mile and a half along those banks, where hundreds of boats docked and disgorged passengers and freight bound for destinations throughout the Northwest. Fort Benton was the world's innermost port, 3495 miles from the Gulf of Mexico.

## Early Explorers

In 1743 the de la Verendrye brothers ventured up the Missouri until they could see the distant mountains which they named the Rockies. No one knows exactly how far the brothers traveled. They may have seen the main chain of the Rockies, or prairie mountains like the Little Rockies, Bears Paw and the Judiths. It is generally felt that Lewis and Clark may have seen the

same mountains when they observed the "Rockies" from a high bluff near Cow Island. The de la Verendrye brothers were the first known whites to enter the upper Missouri; their adventure encouraged the flood of white people into the region during the next century.

## Corps of Discovery

After acquiring the Louisiana Territory that doubled the size of the United States, President Jefferson sent the Lewis and Clark Expedition up the Missouri River in 1804. On their upriver trek the Corps of Discovery's experiences near Fort Benton included their longest stay in any single camp. The Expedition camped at the mouth of Maria's River from June 2 to June 11, 1805. It was there that the decision was made concerning which fork of the river was the true Missouri. No tributary similar to Maria's River had

*Right: Signal Point Bluff is at the lower end of the Fort Benton bottom. Lookouts could see far downriver and signal the coming of steamboats to the people in town.*

*Below: Maria's River flows into the Missouri. Below left is the abandoned site of Ophir; at the upper right is the Lewis and Clark camp June 3 - June 12, 1805.*

been recorded, nor had the Indians downriver mentioned such a large fork. Sacagawea did not recognize the region. With a very high spring rise, Maria's River carried almost as much water as the Missouri and much more silt.

"Which of these rivers was the Missouri?"

June 3, 1805, M. Lewis

The Corps of Discovery camped between the two rivers and explored both. They repaired equip-ment, prepared a cache for heavy items and hid their red pirogue on an island in the trees. To delay any longer was unreasonable, but to take the wrong river could doom the expedition to failure. They must get through the Rockies before winter when the passes were blocked with snow. Most of the men voted for Maria's River; it was muddy like the lower river while the other was flowing clear water.

The night before they left, Lewis and Clark pondered the situation. Their decision was the most critical of the entire journey. The captains went against the opinion of their men. Turning away from the river flowing east from the mountains, they chose the south fork. The State of Montana's Memorial to the Expedition at Fort Benton depicts that crucial decision at the fork of the river. A few days later when Lewis heard the mighty roar of the Great Falls of the Missouri, he realized that they had indeed made the right decision. One of the landmarks known to the expedition before they entered Montana was the series of great cataracts on the Missouri that barred passage further upstream. Lewis sent word back to Captain Clark:

"Inform Capt. C. and the party of my success in finding the falls and settle in their minds all further doubt as to the Missouri."

June 13, 1805, M. Lewis

# Fort Benton's Lewis and Clark

## Decision at the Marias

*The State of Montana's Memorial to the Lewis and Clark Expedition at Fort Benton was dedicated June 13, 1976. The sculpture by Bob Scriver depicts the two Captains, Sacagawea and her baby "Pomp" on a promontory, deciding which channel to follow. It was probably the most critical decision of the journey, and one that helped secure the success of the expedition.*

## Fortunate Meeting

*On July 28, 1806 near the site of Fort Benton, Captain Lewis, Drouillard and the two Field brothers reached the river just in time to meet the rest of their party coming downriver in canoes. They were a welcome sight. It was a fortunate meeting after a harrowing all-night ride from the Two Medicine camp, where they had killed two Blackfoot warriors. Below is Bob Morgan's mural in Fort Benton depicting the meeting on the Fort Benton bottom with Signal Point in the background.*

*Left: Karl Bodmer, artist of the Upper Missouri, accompanied Prince Maximilian of Wied to Fort McKenzie in 1833.*

*Below: Aerial view looking south to the Highwood Mountains showing the black shale bluffs in the area between Fort MacKenzie and Fort Benton. The white rectangle is the site of Fort MacKenzie, one of the Blackfoot trading posts on the Upper Missouri.*

When Lewis and his party arrived at the Fort Benton bottom on their return trip, they were harassed and tired. They had ridden all night following a fight with the Blackfoot at the Two Medicine River. After meeting the rest of the party coming downriver, the men hurriedly opened their cache at Maria's River and departed from Blackfoot country. They left behind a legacy every white man remembered throughout the years of the fur trade . . . life was uneasy in the land of the terrible Blackfoot.

## The Prince and His Artist

The expedition that provided the most scientific account of the upper Missouri occurred in 1833 and 1834. It was led by a German, Prince Maximilian of Wied, and his artist companion Karl Bodmer. In a narrow window of time, from 1831 when the Indians began trade to the small pox

epidemic six years later, the Indian culture remained intact and visible to the whites.

Bodmer, a draftsman and an artist, faithfully recorded not only the Indians and their culture, but also the natural history of the upper river. He produced a beautiful record of the scenery of the upper Missouri. Even today the cliffs and rock formations can be accurately located and compared to Bodmer's work of 1833. The entire collection of Prince Maximilian's journals, including Bodmer's original watercolors and sketches, is at the Joslyn Art Museum in Omaha, Nebraska.

Other expeditions, including artists George Catlin and John James Audubon, came upriver to Fort Union and recorded similar sights. Later Karl Weimar, Alfred Jacob Miller and William Cary depicted early life and scenery of the river above Fort Union.

## Missionaries

The Jesuits were also early travelers on the river. Periodically they made trips downriver from their missions west of the mountains. In 1846 Father Pierre DeSmet and Father Nicholas Point came to Fort Lewis during their journey downriver to St. Louis. Father Point remained throughout the winter and continued downriver in the spring, sketching the fur forts and rock formations of the upper Missouri as he returned to the East.

Father DeSmet returned several more times; other Jesuits established missions in the region to bring Christianity to the Blackfoot. All left behind accounts of the upper river with paint and with pen. Through those descriptions, today we can visualize an animated sketch of history before the first immigrants invaded the high plains.

*Below: Fort Benton's water front in the 1880's when it was Montana's third largest city and the most important transportation center in the Northwest, all because of the river.*

*Chapter 2*

# Beaver and Buffalo

*Fort Benton, established in 1846, was the last Blackfoot fur post, their first agency, and the end of the buffalo and the Blackfoot way of life.*

## Aftermath and Early Fur Trade

Since that eventful day on the Two Medicine when Captain Lewis had his first and only encounter with Indians in Montana, relations between the Blackfoot and the whites were anything but friendly. The Indians killed by Lewis' party were avenged many times over. For over forty years the hair of every free trader hung very loose in Blackfoot country.

It has not been documented that the Corps of Discovery's encounter with the Indians affected relations with the whites in later years. One might be hard pressed not to consider that possibility when reading about the experiences of Jim Bridger, John Coulter, Andrew Henry and other trappers with the "terrible" Blackfoot.

## The Beginning

No official report was ever published of the Lewis and Clark Expedition, probably due to the untimely death of Lewis. However, when Captain Clark returned to St. Louis, rumors began that the upper Missouri abounded in fur-bearing animals. St. Louis, then only a village of a thousand inhabitants, already enjoyed a fur trade of over $100,000. The Expedition's tale certainly piqued the interest of local businessmen.

One businessman in particular was Manuel Lisa, a man of restless energy and a veteran of the fur trade. In 1807 he led an expedition up the Missouri to the mouth of the Yellowstone, and up the Yellowstone to the Big Horn.

*Below: Building Montana's first fur post on the Yellowstone in 1807*

There he established the first fur fort in Montana. Upon his return to St. Louis in 1808, Lisa organized the Missouri Fur Company that operated for a decade on the Yellowstone.

In 1822 the Rocky Mountain Fur Company came to the upper Missouri. They were attacked by the Blackfoot and four men were killed. The survivors retreated downriver and did not return. Several attempts by other companies and free traders to penetrate Blackfoot country in the Three Forks region met with bloody, disastrous results.

John Jacob Astor organized the American Fur Company in 1808; it was the most successful company on the river. After taking in such associates as Pierre Chouteau and Barnard Pratt, the company began to operate in most of the fur country west of the river. In 1827 the company hired Kenneth MacKenzie who was given charge of the upper Missouri. He became the most able trader on the river, often referred to as "King of the Upper Missouri."

MacKenzie built the most prominent trading post on the upper river in 1828. Fort Union,

*Top*: Manuel Lisa built the first fur post in Montana.

*Top left*: Kenneth MacKenzie, bourgeois of Fort Union and "King of the Upper Missouri"

*Bottom*: The American Fur Company's Fort Union, built at the mouth of the Yellow-stone, was the most important fur post from the 1830's until the founding of Fort Benton in 1846.

*Top: Site of Fort Piegan at the mouth of Maria's River*

**Center**: *James Kipp built the first Blackfoot post in 1831.*

**Bottom:** *Piegan village on the Upper Missouri*

situated at the mouth of the Yellowstone, soon became the center of a large successful operation. Most trade centered around the Yellowstone and its tributaries. Aided by James Kipp and Jacob Berger, MacKenzie persuaded the Blackfoot to visit Fort Union in 1830. An agreement was reached that permitted the American Fur Company to establish a trading post in Blackfoot country. The post was only for trade, no free trappers allowed.

## First Blackfoot Post

The following spring James Kipp, with a party of forty-four voyageurs, moved upriver to build the post. When they arrived at the mouth of Maria's River, Kipp's party was met by a large group of Piegans, the southernmost tribe of the Blackfoot. Using his most persuasive powers Kipp convinced the Indians to leave, and return in seventy-five days when the fort was completed and trading could commence. Kipp and his men needed no further incentive to finish the job on time. All were afraid to meet the Indians without the protective walls of the palisade.

Trade at Fort Piegan began with a three-day spree of whiskey and drunken Indians. By the end of the season over 3000 buffalo robes and fur pelts were taken in, a profit of $46,000. When the voyageurs' contract ran out, no one really wanted to stay in Blackfoot country through the winter. Kipp returned with his men, robes and furs to Fort Union. The abandoned fort was burned by the Indians, and the first fur post on the upper Missouri was history.

## Ten Years at MacKenzie

In the spring of 1832 David Mitchell was sent upriver to renew trade with the Blackfoot. Passing the charred remains of Fort Piegan, he brought his keelboat upriver about five miles to a wide bottom on the north side of the

river. There Mitchell built Fort MacKenzie, named in honor of his boss at Fort Union. Fort. MacKenzie was one of the wealthiest and most colorful fur posts in the West.

Alexander Culbertson joined the American Fur Company in 1829 and was their principal trader with the Blackfoot for over thirty years. In 1834 he took command of Fort MacKenzie. Culbertson rebuilt the fort into the most important post in the company. Hailing from Chambersburg, Pennsylvania, Culbertson had great executive ability. With his Blackfoot wife, Natawista, he gained the confidence of the "terrible" Blackfoot; trade improved as did their relations with the whites.

The most detailed account of Indian culture and life at Fort MacKenzie was provided by two visitors to the fort in 1833. Prince Maximilian and artist Karl Bodmer came upriver with Culbertson and stayed at the fort for six weeks.

When the river rose in the spring of 1837, arrival of the keelboats not only brought trade goods for the season but also brought the dreaded disease, smallpox. Indians died by the thousands as smallpox spread through their summer camps. By winter it was estimated that half of their people had perished, decimating the Indian culture to such a degree that it never again was the same.

The American Fur Company was reorganized in 1834. Astor withdrew, Chouteau and Pratt became the principal owners in St. Louis, and MacKenzie be-

*Top: David Mitchell, builder of Fort MacKenzie in 1832, was later an Indian Commissioner on the upper river.*

*Bottom: Site of Fort MacKenzie; the post was burned by the Blackfoot after the massacre. The outline of the fort is ghosted into a present day photo of Brule Bottom.*

*Top: Alexander Culbertson, founder of Fort Benton and Agent-in-Charge of the Upper Missouri*

*Above: Pierre Chouteau Jr., owner of Chouteau and Co.; also called the Upper Missouri Outfit, it was the successor of the American Fur Co.*

came a partner. The new company was known as the Upper Missouri Outfit or Pratt, Chouteau and Company. Culbertson left Fort MacKenzie and assumed control of the entire upper river from Fort Union. With Pratt's death in 1839 the company again reorganized and was called Chouteau and Co. in St. Louis, but remained the UMO in the wilderness.

## The Burning of Fort MacKenzie

Francis A. Chardon succeeded Culbertson in 1841 as factor at Fort MacKenzie. He was an able trader but had a foul disposition. His friend Alexander Harvey was known as the toughest man on the river. Neither man liked Indians. Finding a pig butchered by the Indians, legend has it that they became enraged and went after the perpetrators. A Negro from the fort named Reese was killed, and the stage was set for the ambush and subsequent massacre of Indians at the fort.

The next trading party of Blackfoot arrived at the fort in February 1844 and was invited to trade. While ceremonies were carried on in front of the main gate, from the blockhouse Harvey discharged a cannon loaded with musket shot into the trading party. When the smoke cleared, thirty Indians lay dead or wounded. They were immediately scalped and a victory dance was held that night inside the fort.

The survivors escaped to spread the word. Chardon and company realized the folly of their actions; deep in Blackfoot country in the dead of winter was not a good place for traders in the best of times. Running scared, they abandoned Fort MacKenzie and headed downriver to the mouth of the Judith. Huddled in a temporary structure called Fort F.A.C. or Fort Chardon, the men experienced little trade the next year. The Indians burned the abandoned fort, and trade on the upper river suffered a major setback.

When news of the massacre reached Fort Union, the company immediately sent for Culbertson who was at Fort William on the Laramie straightening out some company affairs. Culbertson came upriver in the fall of 1845 and eventually burned Fort Chardon. Harvey crept downriver with revenge on his mind. David Mitchell and Malcolm Clarke, who accompanied Culbertson, vowed to kill him if Harvey ever showed up again on the upper river. Chardon was ordered to leave Indian country; he was sent to Fort Clark on

*Right: Blackfoot massacre at Fort MacKenzie in the winter of 1842. Harvey fired a cannon into the Indians and Chardon tried to kill the chiefs just inside the gate.*

the lower river and died a few years later.

## Construction of Fort Lewis

Culbertson continued upriver to reestablish trade with the Blackfoot. He bypassed the remains of Fort MacKenzie and stopped at a site three miles above present Fort Benton. On the river's south side at the upper end of Cotton Bottom, Culbertson constructed a wooden palisaded fort. First called Fort Henry then Fort Honore´ Picotte, it was eventually named for Captain Lewis from the Corps of Discovery.

Word went out to the Blackfoot that Culbertson had returned. His apology for the massacre at Fort MacKenzie was accepted and trade resumed immediately. The Indians commented, "The ground has been made good again by Major Culbertson's return and we will not be the first to stain it with blood." The hostile Blackfoot had been calmed, for the time being.

Culbertson again became head of the company on the upper river. Shortly after its completion,

*Below: Fort Lewis, built by Culbertson 1845-1847, from a sketch by Fr. Nicholas Point*

*Top: Fr. Pierre DeSmet held the first Catholic service at Fort Benton in 1846.*

*Below: John Mix Stanley's sketch of Fort Benton in 1853, earliest known view of the fort. Upriver is a Blackfoot trading party and the opposition post of Alexander Harvey's called Fort Campbell.*

Culbertson left Malcolm Clarke in charge of Fort Lewis. After a winter passed, they decided that the site was on the wrong side of the river. It was difficult to reach the fort in the spring and fall due to ice jams and floating ice, and the Indians preferred to camp on the "Sweet Grass"(Teton River). A new location was selected in the fall of 1846. It was downriver, on the other side and closer to the Teton to make trade more convenient for the Blackfoot. The foundations were laid and site preparation occurred that fall, but trade at Fort Lewis went on for another winter.

In the fall of 1846 two Jesuit missionaries arrived at the fort. Father DeSmet and Father Point were from St. Mary's Mission west of the mountains. Father DeSmet's stay was brief, but Father Point remained at Fort Lewis until the following spring. The Jesuits were disappointed in their mission to the Flatheads, and had come east to evangelize the Blackfoot. St. Mary's Mission eventually closed; a white settlement was not reestablished there until 1850 when John Owen built his fort.

## Birthplace of Montana

According to Father Point's journal, on May 19, 1847 the palisades of Fort Lewis were dismantled, floated to the new site and reassembled. Winter trade

proved the value of the change. According to Lieutenant James Bradley's <u>Affairs at Fort Benton</u>, "Not only was the stock of goods completely exhausted, but even bedding, wearing apparel, everything that could be spared from the fort was bartered for the incessant flow of peltries. The collection of robes exceeded twenty thousand."

Called Fort Lewis then Fort Clay, the post was partially constructed of logs. During one of his trips south Culbertson saw buildings made of adobe; he immediately started conversion of the fort to adobe which was warmer and more substantial against gun fire. The engagees were kept busy making adobe bricks from grass collected on the Teton and clay from hills behind the fort.

With completion of the

*Left: Thomas Hart Benton, Senator from Missouri for whom Fort Benton was named*

bourgeois quarters, on Christmas Day in 1850 Culbertson officially named the post Fort Benton in honor of Thomas Hart Benton. He was the U.S. Senator from Missouri who saved the company's license following a dispute with the Federal government concerning whiskey trade with the Indians. In St. Louis the name Fort Benton had been used the previous two years, Culbertson simply made it official.

*Below: Fort Benton in 1855 after reconstruction into adobe. The last fur fort, Fort Benton was the most important in robe trade with the Blackfoot.*

On that Christmas Day Fort Benton was born, the longest existing white settlement in Montana, its birthplace and most historic city.

## Rival Opposition

Trade continued to improve during the ensuing years and Chouteau and Company prospered. Other businessmen in St. Louis became interested in the upper river trade. In 1842 Bolton, Fox, Cotton and Livingston organized the Union Fur Company. They first established Fort Mortimer at the mouth of the Yellowstone. Two small fur forts were established farther upstream near the present site of Fort Benton. Fort Cotton was built on the south bank upriver from Fort Benton, and Fort Fox-Livingston was just below Fort MacKenzie. Both existed only one season before being abandoned. The Union Fur Company sold out to Chouteau and Company in 1845, and all opposition disappeared from the upper river.

## Harvey's Revenge

Alexander Harvey was probably the wildest, meanest trader on the upper river. Not at all concerned about the death threats issued by Mitchell and Clarke, Harvey took on the American Fur Company in St. Louis law courts and caused the company a great deal of trouble with the Federal government. With several other disgruntled former employees, he organized an opposition firm. Harvey, Primeau, Bois and Picotte were financially supported by Robert Campbell, American Fur's old nemesis of the 1830's on the lower river and in the mountains. They formed the St. Louis

Fur Company, usually referred to as Harvey, Primeau and Company.

Harvey charged upriver in the spring of 1846 with forty-five men from St. Louis, and hired fifty more men along the way. With experienced traders and financial backing, they were a formidable challenge to the established company. Harvey was determined to make his presence felt on the upper Missouri.

His group stopped near Fort Union only long enough to build mackinaws. Just below the mouth of Shonkin Creek on the south bank of the Missouri, Harvey constructed a small log enclosure called Harvey's Trading Post. In 1847 he moved upriver to the same bottom as Fort Benton, and built an adobe fort called Fort Campbell a mile from its rival. Business was good until Harvey's death, but in 1860 the opposition gave up and was sold to Chouteau and Company. Fort Campbell was a Jesuit monastery for a short time, a shocking change from the wild and wooly fur post.

## Last Years of the Fur Trade

Under the careful tutelage of Scotsman Andrew Dawson as factor, for more than fifteen years Fort Benton was the premier trading post in Blackfoot country. The fort's log walls and buildings had gradually been replaced by adobe; work was finally finished in 1860. The adobe blocks were 4x8x16 and created a wall 28"

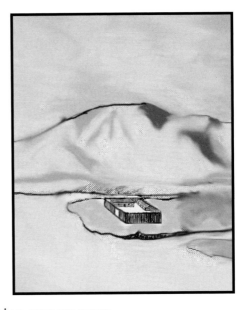

thick. On opposing corners were two bastions. Buildings inside the fort were constructed to face the courtyard; their back walls formed part of the 14-foot palisades. A large double gate topped with a huge mural fronted the river.

The major problem with adobe construction in this country was maintenance. Less than ten years after completion, the walls and buildings of Fort Benton were sagging. When the military arrived in 1869, the fort was in such poor condition that quarters for most of the men were found elsewhere.

Unlike Fort MacKenzie that had double gates with a trading area between, Fort Benton had a unique trade store. A narrow

**Top:** *Mackinaw boats leaving Fort Benton in the spring with robes taken during the past year's trading season*

***Middle:*** *Located below Fort MacKenzie on the Missouri, the Union Fur Co.'s Fort Fox-Livingston existed only one trade season.*

*Right:* Andrew Dawson, long-time factor at Fort Benton after Alexander Culbertson left

*Below:* A keelboat being poled up the Missouri to Fort Benton with next year's trade goods

pathway allowed only a few Indians into the store at any one time; the passage was commanded by a gun port through the adobe wall. Only one trader at a time was accommodated at the trade window. Such security measures discouraged any violence during trading. After a number of years with hostilities at a minimum, the trade store was opened to the outside. Windows and doors were cut and a long porch was built overlooking the river. Trade flourished as successive factors, from Clarke to Dawson to Baker, made money in the buffalo robe trade. The annual take rose to over fifty thousand robes, worth from $4.50 to $5.00 each in St. Louis.

The garrison of a fur fort consisted of the bourgeois or factor (usually referred to as "Major"), clerk, interpreter, cook, carpenters, blacksmiths, hunters, and from fifty to seventy-five engagees. For a fifteen-month contract the men received two hundred dollars, food and quarters. Meals were prepared and served in the big kitchen. Those with a vocation received higher wages; clerks earned from $500 to $1000 and were hired for one to three years. They enjoyed the privilege of the bourgeois dining table, which had more variety, and the prospect of becoming a partner in the firm.

Culbertson made frequent trips to St. Louis and to Fort Benton. With a load of freight from St. Louis, in 1851 Culbertson and five other men blazed a wagon road around the north side of the Bears Paw. It became a well-used route during the gold rush days. Culbertson's was the first wheeled vehicle that transported freight to Fort Benton, initiating a trade era that lasted to the turn-of-the-century.

## The Way West

Through the vast prairie ran the Missouri River, a waterway from St. Louis to the Rocky Mountains. It was treacherous, full of snags, sandbars, and rapids, but it was still the fastest and safest means of transportation into the great fur trading region.

At first only small boats were used, such as dugout canoes and bullboats. As trade increased, companies began to use keelboats like those on the Ohio and the Mississippi. Keelboats were large and required a great deal of manpower to move against the current. They had a sail, but only in a few places did the wind blow in the right direction. The crew sometimes oared or poled the boat. Much of the power came from cordelling, a back-breaking exertion. With long lines attached to the mast and the bow, men in the water or along the bank pulled the two- or three-ton boat against the current. A special type of man, with tough feet and determination almost beyond belief, worked the river between Fort Union and Fort Benton. The voyageurs were a hardy breed; their resilience was the substance of the fur trade.

Fur posts moved further and further up the river followed by the fleet of boats. The head of navigation moved toward the mountains until it reached Fort Benton.

Steamboats followed the fur trade upriver but at a much slower pace, reaching Fort Union in 1832. The first mountain boat was the *Yellowstone*. It was owned by the American Fur Company and operated between St. Louis and the forts upriver. The *Yellowstone* supplied the fur posts in the spring and brought the winter furs and robes downriver to Eastern markets. The *El Paso* arrived at the mouth of the Milk River in 1850, but it was another ten years before

*Below: Fort Benton in 1856, with a Blackfoot encampment and a small flat-bottomed boat about to unload supplies for the next year's robe trade*

*Above: After arrival of the steamboat, a primitive town began to grow between Fort Benton and Forts Campbell and LaBarge upriver. Sketch by Granville Stuart*

steamboats reached Fort Benton.

In the spring the levee in front of Fort Benton may have two or more keelboats tied up and a flotilla of other small craft. On the opposite bank mackinaws were under construction for the trip to St. Louis with the winter's take. Built in the chantier or boatyard, mackinaws were constructed of rough-sawn lumber from the Highwood Mountains. They were used only for a single voyage downriver to St. Louis where they were dismantled and the lumber was sold. The flat-bottomed mackinaw had a rear sweep for steering; there was usually a small cabin in the rear. When it headed for the States, the boat was completely filled with robes, furs and passengers.

## Manifest Destiny

Wagons began to roll westward to Oregon in 1843. James Polk was elected President in 1844 with the slogan "Fifty-four Forty or Fight." Manifest Destiny pushed U.S. borders to the Pacific in the Northwest and in California. President Polk was the greatest expansionist since Thomas Jefferson. Following the 1846 border settlement with Great Britain at the 49th parallel, land north of the Columbia River became new U.S. territory. Sweeping changes in the boundaries triggered a second surge of western exploration by the Federal government.

In March 1853 the Territory of Washington was created from the Pacific Coast to the crest of the Rockies. Major Isaac Stevens, a young Mexican War veteran, became governor of the new territory. He was commissioned to negotiate peace treaties with the Indians, find a wagon route west and a northern route for a transcontinental railroad.

Steven's expedition departed from Fort Snelling, near St. Paul, Minnesota. The party included surveyors, scientists and John Mix Stanley, artist and photographer. They crossed the northern prairies to Fort Union at the mouth of the Yellowstone.

Accompanied by Alexander Culbertson, the expedition arrived at Fort Benton via the wagon route established by Culbertson two years earlier.

During his three weeks in Fort Benton, Stevens organized several meetings with Indians from the area. In September he met with Blackfoot chiefs at Fort Benton, the first formal council of the Blackfoot and the U.S. government. Shortly thereafter Stevens proceeded to the coast, sending Culbertson and Lieutenant Saxton to Washington D.C. for more money; his $40,000 had run out. Stevens' able lieutenant John Mullan remained in Fort Benton to explore routes through the mountains. Mullan spent a year exploring the area between Fort Benton and Fort Owen on the Bitterroot. The route he chose became the first leg of the Mullan Road to the

Columbia.

In 1854 the Federal government established the Nebraska Territory. For the first time Fort Benton officially had sovereignty in the United States as part of that territory.

## Indian Treaty of 1855

The great Indian treaty held near Fort Benton occurred in the fall of 1855 after many delays. Stevens returned from Olympia in

*Top: Lt. John Mullan, builder of the first Federal road in the Northwest*

*Bottom: Fort Benton in the days before the steamboat, when the year's supplies arrived by keelboat after a long arduous trip upriver from St. Louis*

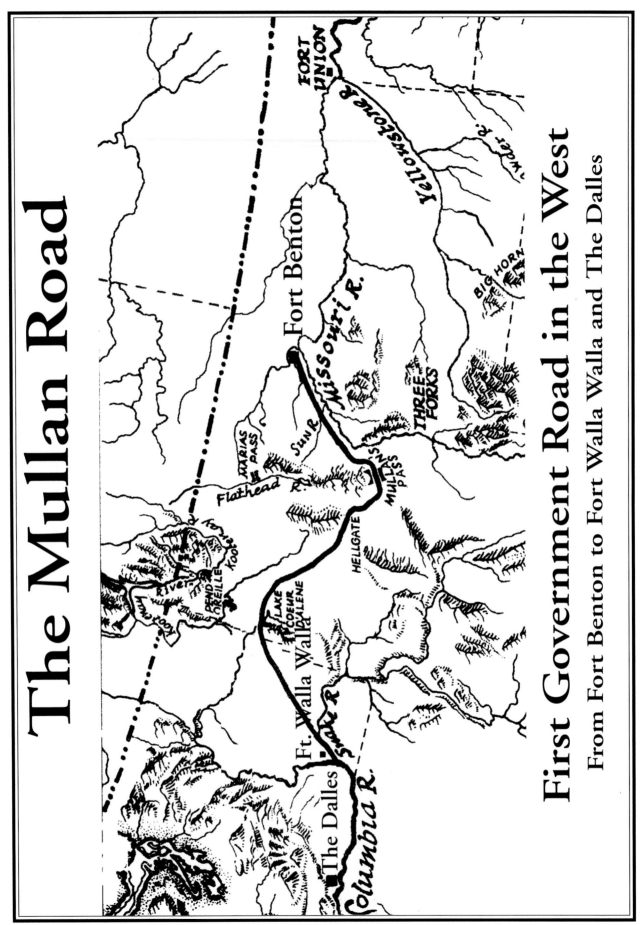

# The Mullan Road

## First Government Road in the West

From Fort Benton to Fort Walla Walla and The Dalles

July. Alfred Cummings, the newly-appointed Commissioner of Indian Affairs, left St. Louis in June, two months after the spring rise. His trip was a series of missed deadlines, partially attributed to the ponderous size of the 350-pound commissioner! Henry Kennerly, the commissioner's clerk, reported that they could not reach Fort Benton until October. The Indians, encamped for almost a month, were anxious to begin the fall hunt and were threatening to leave. The decision was made to move the treaty site to the mouth of the Judith, about ninety miles closer to the party coming upriver. Finally the council was held and after several days the treaty was signed on October 17, 1855.

The Blackfoot confederation and the Gros Ventres agreed to keep peace with the Salish and Nez Perce west of the mountains, and to permit their fall buffalo hunt on the plains. For years the hunt had been a traumatic experience for the western tribes; the

Blackfoot continually counted coup, making life miserable until they returned home. The confederation also agreed to stop warring with their bitter enemies: the Crow, Assiniboine, and Sioux. When the great Indian council at the Judith ended, some 3500 Indians with new blankets, beads, and calico, went off to their fall

*Above: 1855 Blackfoot treaty site at the mouth of the Judith River. Under the canopy in the center is Gov. Stevens; seated is Alfred Cummings; in the back left is Alexander Culbertson. Drawing by Gustav Sohon*

*Left: Isaac I. Stevens: Civil War hero, newly-appointed governor of the Washington Territory and architect of the Blackfoot Treaty of 1855*

31

hunt and twenty-five years of ill treatment by the U.S. government.

That same year Fort Benton became the first Blackfoot Indian Agency for the U.S. government. An Indian agent was appointed and quartered in the fort. His duties were to disperse annuities to the tribes of the Blackfoot Nation and to maintain peaceful relations between them and the white population in Montana.

## Mullan Builds a Road

In 1859-1860 Lieutenant John Mullan completed his military road. It ran between Fort Walla Walla on the big bend of the Columbia across the mountains to Fort Benton on the Missouri, establishing a northern water and land route to the Pacific. After two years of exploring the Rockies and several delays including an Indian war, Lieutenant Mullan started to build the road from Fort Walla Walla in

*Below: The Chippewa, first steamboat to reach Fort Benton and establish it as head of navigation on the Missouri River in 1860*

1859. Following a winter in the Rockies he reached Hellgate near Missoula in June 1860 and joined up with the first segment he began in Fort Benton. The Mullan Road was finished just in time for Major Blake to move three hundred men to Washington Territory with considerable savings to the Federal government. They arrived in Fort Benton aboard the *Key West,* the second steamboat to reach that far up the Missouri.

The cost of Mullan's road was $230,000. Although it was seldom used by the military, it was the main route for immigrants to the Northwest and for miners headed to northern Idaho's gold fields. In 1978 this first Federal road in the West was designated as a National Historic Civil Engineer-

ing Landmark. The 624-mile route ushered in Fort Benton's emergence from a fur trading post to a river port on the upper Missouri. Today the route is marked with marble obelisks depicting Mullan in relief. One stands at the beginning of the road on the levee in Fort Benton.

## Two Momentous Events

A stranger named John Silverthorne showed up at the trade store in Fort Benton during the spring of 1858. He traded gold dust for $1000 worth of goods. Silverthorne obtained the gold dust by trading with Findlay at Benetsee's Creek (later Gold Creek near Deer Lodge). The mountain creeks of Montana were "showing

*Top: Fort Benton levee in June 1860 with the first steamboats, Chippewa and Key West. Major Blake's troops camped below the fort prior to their departure on the first wagon train over the Mullan Road.*

*Middle: Charles Chouteau brought the first two steamboats to Fort Benton.*

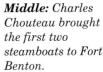

*Left: Gustav Sohon, artist with Mullan's party, sketched Fort Benton in 1860 on their arrival after completing the wagon road.*

*Above: Fort Benton in 1860, a sketch from a photo by J.D. Hutton, photographer for the Raynolds Expedition*

color" and the gold rush was only a heartbeat away.

The next spring John LaBarge and Charles Chouteau brought the steamboat *Chippewa* to Brule Bottom, named for the

charred ruins of Fort MacKenzie, where they ran out of fuel and were forced to unload. In 1860 LaBarge brought the steamers *Chippewa* and *Key West* all the way to Fort Benton. A new head of navigation was established on the Missouri River, and Fort Benton became the world's innermost port.

Those two events triggered the mass immigration of people into Montana seeking gold. The discovery on Grasshopper Creek in the mountains to the south helped open the newly-acquired U.S. territory in the Northwest.

*Middle: Fort Benton looking upriver with Blockhouse and Engagees Quarters*

*Right: After the military left in 1881, Fort Benton was in ruins. Building on the right was military headquarters.*

*Chapter 3*

# Tough Town

*GOLD! brought them from all corners of the country, all walks of life, and for only one reason, . . . "to see the elephant"*

## Birth of a Town

The first steamboats arrived in Fort Benton when beaver hats were out of style and the fur trade had turned to buffalo robes and wolf pelts. In 1861, a few years after that first exchange in gold dust at the fort, James and Granville Stuart reported gold discoveries in the Deer Lodge Valley.

Fort Benton was only a walled fortification. John Largent commented in his journal in the spring of 1862 that there were still no buildings outside the fort. Log and adobe structures were erected upriver later that year, and a town was born.

## Culbertson Leaves

Alexander Culbertson retired from the American Fur Company in 1861 with a fortune of over $400,000, and took up residence with his Blackfoot wife Natawista in Peoria, Illinois. He built a beautiful home and lived

well for a few years, then was hit by bankruptcy and lost his savings. Culbertson returned to the river and made several trips to Fort Benton, where he was interviewed by Lt. James Bradley. Most of the material in Bradley's manuscript, Affairs at Fort Benton, came from those interviews.

Natawista went to the Blood Reservation in Canada

*Top: Natawista Iksana, Blood wife of Alexander Culbertson and sister of Crowfoot*

35

*Top*: St. Louis advertisement for LaBarge, Harkness & Co.

*Top right*: Captain Joseph LaBarge

*Bottom*: Fort LaBarge in 1862 with the Emilie docked at the upper levee; the fort was only warehouses and offices.

where she lived out the rest of her life with her people. Culbertson spent his last days in Orleans, Nebraska, with his daughter Julia; he died on August 27, 1879. Culbertson's grave and monument are located in the Orleans cemetery.

## The Last Opposition

During the spring of 1862 the last opposition company was organized to tap the prospective gold trade. Promoters were Joseph and John LaBarge, famous river pilots, James Harkness and three others. With the LaBarge brothers at their helms, two steamboats, the *Emilie* and the *Shreveport*, raced upriver against two American Fur Company boats, the *Key West* and the *Spread Eagle*. The *Spread Eagle* replaced the *Chippewa* which had blown up at the mouth of Poplar Creek the previous spring. Arriving three days ahead of the company boats, the LaBarge boys docked upriver from old Fort Campbell. They constructed a three-sided enclosure facing the

river and called it Fort LaBarge. Aboard their boats were a grist mill, a saw mill and 400 miners. The rush was on. Harkness went to Deer Lodge where he set up a company trading post near the diggings.

That same year James L. Fisk brought 130 people to the West. Fifty guards accompanied their wagon train from Minnesota, following the route of Stevens and Culbertson to Fort Benton. The group arrived in September then traveled Mullan's road to the gold fields of southwestern Montana.

The word "gold" spread across the frontier like wildfire. People dropped everything and came from everywhere to make their fortunes. They traveled thousands of miles often under adverse conditions to stake a claim and strike it rich. Some came by wagon, some walked, but most came by steamboat up the Missouri. All sought Utopia in the mountains of Montana. Over three-quarters of the miners who reached Montana during the gold rush passed through Fort Benton either coming or going.

## Moving Out on the Flat

Big gold strikes at Bannack and Grasshopper Creek in 1862 brought a flood of humanity on every boat, accompanied by supplies, mining equipment and food stuffs. There were millions to be made, not only by miners but also by merchants, freighters and gamblers, all seeking their share of the riches.

The levee received so much freight in 1862 that it was stacked in great piles, waiting for wagons to transport it overland. 1863 was a low-water year and no steamboats reached Fort Benton, the ruination of the new opposition company; on August 31 Fort

*Top: Spread Eagle, the last steamboat owned by the American Fur Co.*

*Bottom: Fort Benton levee in the spring of 1867, the oldest known photo of Front Street*

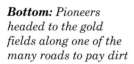

*Top: Front Street 1868 during the freighting season at the height of gold rush*

LaBarge became American Fur Company property. The placers yielded eight million dollars that year. Most miners returned to the States by mackinaw, after first parting with some of their dust in Fort Benton's ramshackle saloons, brothels and gambling houses.

The site of Fort Benton was first part of the Louisiana Purchase, then the Missouri and Nebraska Territories. In 1861 the Dakota Territory was carved from Nebraska. Two years later Idaho Territory claimed the land from Dakota east of the mountains where the fort was located. The final change in 1864 established the Montana Territory. Since its founding, Fort Benton saw five territorial changes.

The gold rush triggered a building boom in Fort Benton. A few log cabins sprouted up across

*Bottom: Pioneers headed to the gold fields along one of the many roads to pay dirt*

38

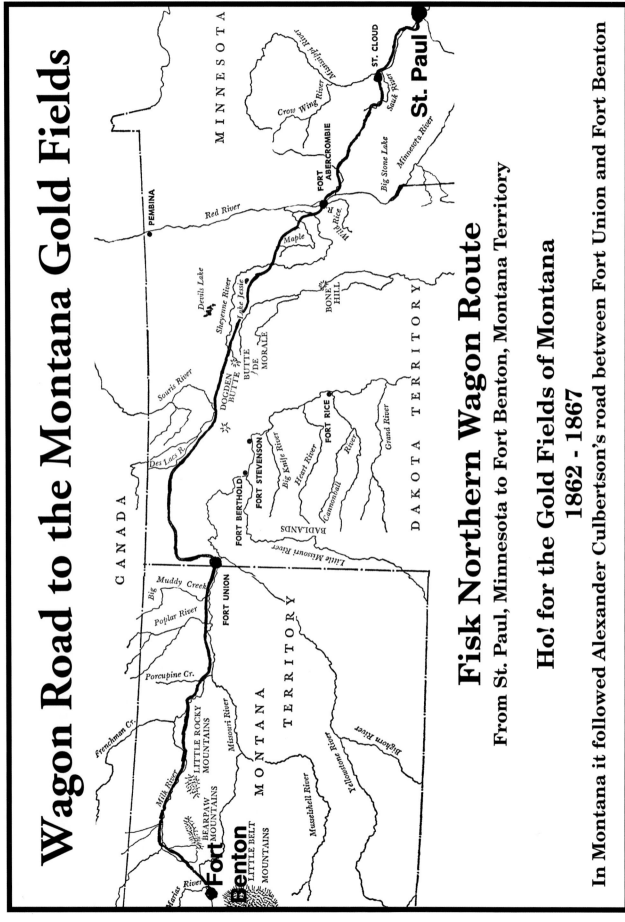

# Wagon Road to the Montana Gold Fields

## Fisk Northern Wagon Route

**From St. Paul, Minnesota to Fort Benton, Montana Territory**

### Ho! for the Gold Fields of Montana
### 1862 - 1867

In Montana it followed Alexander Culbertson's road between Fort Union and Fort Benton

*Above: The mile-long levee piled high with freight bound for the gold fields in the mountains*

the flat from the fort. On Front Street the first mercantile business was constructed of cottonwood logs by Mercure and Laurion. It housed Carroll, Steell and Co., the first of several great trading firms that headquartered in Fort Benton. A single row of permanent saloons, brothels, gambling houses and other commercial enterprises sprang up along the levee.

Often only smokestacks of the steamboats were visible above

the mountains of crates, barrels and cartons stacked on the levee. The heavily rutted street was dangerous to negotiate as many teams of wagons made their way toward Helena Hill and the gold fields in the mountains to the southwest.

With the Civil War in the East, law and order on the northern frontier was nonexistent. There were no troops available to quell an Indian uprising, no marshals to enforce the law, and no courts to try the offenders. Vigilantes took over in the gold camps, but in the river town with its transient population it was "everyone for himself and the devil takes the hindmost."

*Right: Front Street in the 1860's during the freighting season with Murphy Neel and Carroll & Steell stores*

# Benton to Helena Stage Road

*Left: 28 Mile Springs Station, operated by Ed Kelly, was where horses were changed. It was only 28 miles to Fort Benton.*

*Below: Birdtail Divide; it was a night trip over the top after leaving Eagle Rock Station at midnight.*

*Insert: Birdtail Rock, a landmark along the route*

*Below: Rock Creek Station and breakfast with the Green family after the all-night ride over the Birdtail*

*Left: Changing horses at Sun River Leavings while passengers wait on board*

*Above: Eagle Rock Station, a night stop up the Birdtail, was operated by August Nage and his family.*

41

*Above: Bull team headed out of Fort Benton up the Mullan Road to Helena or Virginia City*

*Top right: Matt Carroll and George Steell, founders of the first commercial business in Fort Benton and part-owners of the Diamond R Freighting Company*

*Right: Helena to Fort Benton stage; the mud wagon was used during wet weather instead of the heavier Concord coaches.*

## Ho! for the Gold Fields

Three wagons on short hitches were pulled by ten yokes of oxen or sixteen mules, urged on by the raucous voices of bullwhackers and mule skinners. Their vocabulary was astonishing! Up the steep trail out of the river bottom their animals pulled as much as twenty tons of freight.

Trails went from Fort Benton in many directions, but during the 1860's the most traveled was the Mullan Road to Last Chance, Virginia City and Bannack. The trail led across the prairie to Bull Coulee and 28-Mile Springs, over the flats by Benton Lake and down into the valley of the Sun River. Fort Shaw was in the distance as the trail went up the Bird Tail and continued to the Dearborn. The worst stretch was over the mountains to Sieben. Eventually a toll road was built along Little Prickly Pear Canyon following the creek to Silver City. From there the Mullan Road skirted the Scratch Gravel Hills to Helena, ten days and 140 miles later. Many wagons continued on through the mountains and valleys of the Rockies to Virginia City and Bannack, delivering their wares to merchants in the gold camps.

The stage followed the same route as the wagon trains, but the trip took just two days and two nights. Horses were changed at three stops; three drivers drove three sections of the trail. The

# Wagon and Stage Road to the Gold Fields out of Fort Benton

## Including Helena-Fort Benton Stage Stations

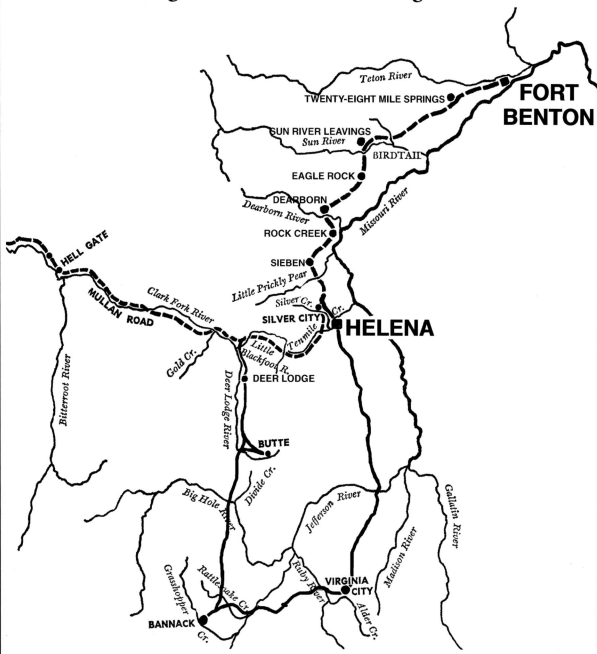

## From Fort Benton to Helena, Virginia City and Bannack 1862 - 1869

*Right:* Four-horse hitch on a mud wagon of the Benton-Helena Stage Line

*Below:* First I.G. Baker store on Front Street, 1866; became Montana's largest mercantile

stage ran every other day from Fort Benton to Helena. It was first operated by Wells Fargo, later by Gilmer and Salisbury, then locally-owned by T.C. Power and Bro.

## Mercantiles Along the Levee

I. G. Baker, the last factor at the fort, moved downtown into a log store in 1866. Before the turn-of-the-century his enterprise became the largest mercantile business in the Northwest. The Baker empire eventually spread from Edmonton and the Great Slave Lake in the north to the Gulf and St. Louis in the south, and into the financial centers of New

York and Montreal in the east. His wagons and stores were found in thousands of square miles in Canada and in the territories of Montana, Idaho, Washington and the Dakotas.

In 1867 the Conrad brothers arrived. William and Charles were Southern Civil War veterans from a bankrupt family plantation in Virginia. They stepped ashore in Fort Benton with only a silver dollar between them. The Conrads joined Baker's company, became a driving force in the West, and in just twenty-five years parleyed that dollar into millions.

The year after Baker built his store, another young Virginian

reached Fort Benton with a supply of goods to start his business. T.C. Power needed a place to store his wares; I.G. Baker gallantly furnished him with a tent on the levee. During the next two decades the men became not only friendly rivals, but also partners in several ventures. T.C. Power and Bro.

*Above: T.H. Kleinschmidt with his brother built a large concrete warehouse and store in 1877, but had a business in Fort Benton since the 1860's.*

*Above left: Isaac G. Baker, founder of the largest mercantile business in Montana's history*

*Below: Upper levee with Murphy, Neel Co. warehouses and a bull team headed for the gold fields*

*Left*: *William G. Conrad ran the Fort Benton enterprises for the I.G. Baker Co.*

*Right*: *Charles E. Conrad ran Baker interests in Canada during the early years of the whiskey trade.*

grew into a giant corporation, with steamboats, wagons, stagecoaches and stores scattered across the northwestern U.S. and Canada.

Other mercantile businesses that competed with the two giants were Carroll and Steell, Murphy, Neel and Co. (later Murphy Maclay), W.S. Wetzel and Co. and Kleinschmidt and Bro. Those firms ran wagons and had stores in the territories but never expanded into Canadian trade.

*Right*: *T.C. Power & Bro.'s first store on Front Street, after doing business in a borrowed tent for the first year*

46

# Steamboats of the Gold Rush

*Below:* Steamer Red Cloud; she was the fastest boat on the river during the gold rush.

*Above left:* Steamboat DeSmet, named for the Jesuit missionary, was a side-wheeler.

*Above:* Sanford Coulson, owner of the largest transportation company on the upper river in the 1860's-1870's

*Right:* Montana, flagship of the Coulson Line and the largest boat on the river, made only one trip to Fort Benton.

*Left:* Grant Marsh, finest pilot on the Upper Missouri

*Right:* First Benton docked at the levee

## Water and Land Transportation

Several shipping companies grew up in the territory and freighted from Fort Benton. The Coulson Steamboat Line was the major river company. It operated over twenty-five boats including the three largest on the upper river: the *Montana*, *Dacotah* and *Wyoming*. The boats were 252 feet long and carried 650 tons of freight.

The Diamond R Transportation Company began in 1863. By 1868, with investment money from Charles Broadwater in Helena and Carroll and Steell in Fort Benton, it had grown into the biggest freight wagon outfit in the territory. The company owned over one hundred Murphy wagons and several hundred head of mules, horses and oxen.

Through the 1860's river traffic increased rapidly; only low water slowed the flow of goods upriver from St. Louis. According to their size, river boats could carry from 100 tons to 600 tons of freight. It took over a month to make the trip upriver and less than half that time to return. In 1866 the *Luella* took down a wagon load of gold belonging to 230

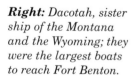

*Top: Uptown businesses: Overland Hotel run by Bill Hamilton; Carroll & Steell, mercantile; and the stage station for Wells Fargo*

*Inset: Bill Hamilton: Indian fighter, frontiersman and early entrepreneur*

*Right: Dacotah, sister ship of the Montana and the Wyoming; they were the largest boats to reach Fort Benton.*

miners . . . valued at one and a half million dollars. During the big placer years 1867-1868, over 24 million dollars in gold went downriver on steamboats. Profits for river men were also astronomical, in some cases as much as $40,000 to $100,000 for one trip.

Passengers paid $150 for the journey from St. Louis; they slept on the deck and were expected to help haul wood. The decks were filled with freight, at 8 to 15 dollars per hundred weight to Fort Benton, which was hauled by wagon to Bannack, Virginia City and Helena for 6 cents a pound.

Everyone charged high prices for goods and services in this wilderness, but gold dust was plentiful and no one questioned the tariff. The river boat freighting business realized three million dollars profit in 1867. 1868 and 1869 were the biggest years of the placers in Montana.

*Top:* Two Diamond R freight outfits on Main Street, ready to leave Fort Benton

*Below:* Col. Clendenin, agent-in-charge for the Coulson Lines, posed with freight on the upper levee during the 1860's.

CHOTEAU HOUSE.

*Top: Thwing House, built in 1868 by Baker and Power interests, became the Choteau House.*

*Below: Bloodiest Block in later years when Fort Benton had attained respectability*

## Uptown, Downtown

Many of Fort Benton's tents and log structures were replaced or at least received false fronts and siding. The early commercial district was upriver from the site of the old bridge. It contained the Overland Hotel, run by Bill Hamilton, and establishments owned by Carroll and Steell, Murphy Neel and W. S. Wetzel. Wells Fargo was also an upriver business. The hotel furnished fine cuisine and provided comfortable rooms in the back of its single-story structure.

When Baker and Power opened their enterprises down river near the fort, competition developed between the two commercial districts. Baker and Power entered into their first joint venture when they built the Thwing House, later called the Choteau House, between their establishments. Run by Mrs. Thwing, it was an eatery and hostelry. Baker and Power urged Hans Wackerlin to construct a hardware and tinsmith business nearby. Separated by the "bloodiest block in the West," successful businesses grew up at both ends of Front Street in the 1860's.

The most publicized block in early Fort Benton was between Baker and St. John's Streets. It was an area one entered knowing that without provocation your poke could be lost at the very least, and your life at the very most. For over ten years the block averaged three killings per month, with no arrests and only one or two hangings. Fort Benton definitely was a town with "hair" on it.

## Booze, Bars and Brothels

Miners always spent a few days in Fort Benton at both ends of

# Bloodiest Block

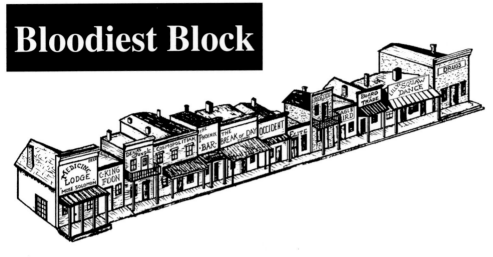

**Top:** *Bloodiest Block in the West in 1867, open twenty-four hours a day where anything was legal during the gold rush days*

their river trip. It took time to arrange overland transport to the gold fields and a river boat to the States when winter approached. To relieve their boredom, an array of bars, dance halls and brothels served booze twenty-four hours a day. From early spring until the first snow, gambling houses removed dust from the miner's poke. Betting limits were from the floor to the ceiling in all establishments.

Owners and operators of gambling enterprises followed gold strikes throughout the West, relieving many miners of their summer earnings before they returned to the States. Faro, black jack, poker and craps did their part; rot gut whiskey, a cut above that sold to the Indians, captured its share. Ladies-of-the-night finished off many a miner's poke before he boarded the boat to St. Louis. Kamoose Taylor, free trader and bar owner, had a saying that was generally accepted among all the saloons on Front Street, "In God we trust, all others cash."

The most infamous owner was Eleanor Dumont, alias Madame Moustache. She packed two revolvers and is credited with

chasing off a steamboat laden with smallpox. Eleanor's Cosmopolitan was one of the most popular saloons. She played blackjack at a raised corner table, and served booze and girls to all takers. Other disreputable institutions along Front Street were Dena Murray's Jungle, Mose Solomon's Medicine Lodge, the Break-of-Day Saloon, the Squaw Dance and the Board of Trade. All prospered during the 1860's when thousands of miners, traders, mule skinners and bullwhackers came through their swinging doors.

**Left:** *Eleanor DuMont, alias Madame Moustache, gambler and madame in most of the gold camps of the West*

51

The list of those who passed through Fort Benton reads like a who's who of notable Western characters. Gunmen, bank robbers and miners came upriver. Quantrill's Raiders paid a visit along with Frank and Jesse James and other members of the Missouri gangs. At the close of the Civil War veterans of both armies headed for the gold fields. The aftermath of the war sometimes spilled out onto Front Street. It was the busiest street in the territory, running twenty-four hours a day from high water in early spring until the river froze over in the winter. Advice often given to a greenhorn when he stepped off a riverboat was, "It's a tough town. Keep your mouth shut and walk down the middle of the street." Fort Benton was a refuge for many with a price on their heads. People came and went, no questions asked.

## Fourth of July, Fort Benton Style

On the Fourth of July at the end of the Civil War in 1865 William Gladstone commented, "I shall never forget the 4th of July in Benton. Most of the men were from the Southern army and their hatred of the North expressed itself in an unmistakable way. There were 1500 men in Benton and I saw such desperate characters as the James brothers among them. You can imagine the fights and rows that went on that day. With feelings of mutual hate, inflamed by bad whiskey, the men of the North and South were only too eager to come to blows. It was hell upon earth for a time."

## HooDoo No. 25

The curse of the HooDoo began in the town's early years with the hanging of Billy Hensel, a self-appointed marshal. Hensel came to Fort Benton after "beating the rap" in Helena for the murder of a Chinese woman. He immediately made friends and began to promote the need for a marshal. No law of any kind existed in this frontier Missouri River port. By public acclaim Hensel put on a

*Left: HooDoo Block #25 on Main Street, with log jail and gallows, in the 1860's*

badge and initiated nightly patrols on the streets and in the back alleys. However, it seems that the crime rate, especially robberies of drunks, rapidly increased after the new marshal assumed his duties.

At Hensel's insistence a Vigilance Committee was established to aid the marshal's efforts, but became suspicious of him and set a trap. One evening Hensel was told that the committee had discovered the robber, and asked if he had a rope for the hanging. "No," he replied, "but I can get one mighty quick." He hurried down the street to the nearest mercantile and purchased the necessary length of manila hemp for the job. When he rejoined the crowd he called out, "Where is the S.O.B.? Show him to me!" A giant of a man from the Vigilance Committee stepped forward and clamped his hand on the marshal's shoulder, saying "Here he is, right here." They dragged Hensel off to the gallows that stood next to the little log jail on Block #25. He was hanged with his own rope and left dangling well into the next day, the victim of his own scheme. The evil legend of Block #25 began.

For years the property was called the HooDoo Block, the scene of most tragedies that befell this little town. Following an Indian attack, a squaw man hid his father-in-law until he was discovered the next morning by the local

*Bottom: Wagons, usually in tandems of three, were pulled to the gold fields by horses, mules or oxen; these five were smaller than the big Murphy's and were pulled by seven teams of horses. Note that the driver was not seated in the wagon but rode one of the wheel horses.*

53

*Right: Granville Stuart's drawing of the abandoned town of Ophir; Missouri R. on right and Maria's R. along far hills to the left*

citizenry. The Indian was immediately dragged off to the gallows on Block 25 and hanged. Three drunken soldiers were jailed for shooting up the town. That night the jail burned, killing the soldiers.

A few years later a livery was built on the empty block and a well was dug out back. When Mountain Chief's son was shot on Front Street, they dumped his body into the well. The practice continued for years, creating the legend of the Golgotha well or the place of skulls. The livery owner ignored the curse and built a house. Shortly after its completion his wife died suddenly; he died a few weeks later, then the house burned to the ground.

In later years a furniture store was built on the opposite corner at Bond and Main Street by Ferdinand C. Roosevelt. While under construction, it blew down during a terrible wind storm, the only building in town affected by the storm. The store eventually

caught fire and burned, along with the newly-built I.O.O.F. Hall nearby. The last chapter was written when the livery burned, leaving the block empty except for the body-filled well.

The HooDoo Block stood vacant until the old stories died. By the turn-of-the-century its luck had changed and new buildings went up. Old timers agreed that the HooDoo had exhausted its power for evil. Today there are nine buildings on Block 25, and there have been no fires or death in years.

## Indian Trouble

As white men traveled to the gold fields, some lost their scalps along the way to the Blackfoot. Others were killed in their isolated cabins; lone traders and trappers were not safe in Blackfoot country. Throughout the fur trade period, people lived within the safe confines of the fort or traveled in groups for protection. Sometimes that was not enough. Incidents continued even after townspeople moved onto the flats near the fort.

In 1864 plans were made to build a port to rival Fort Benton at the confluence of the Marias and Missouri. Construction of Ophir began in the spring of 1865. A few log structures were up by May 25, when ten woodcutters ventured up the Marias to cut logs. They encountered a band of Bloods led by Calf Shirt, and all ten woodcutters were soon dispatched to the Promised Land. Plans for the new port were quickly abandoned.

The experience of Jerry Potts, later a guide for the North West Mounted Police, was typical of the unrest between whites and Indians. Out on the Shonkin, Potts ran into a Crow war party who forced him to accompany them. Potts, who understood the Crow tongue, soon realized that the Indians planned to kill him. When the locks of their guns clicked, Potts slid from his horse and killed four of them as he fell to the ground. He returned to Fort Benton for help from his Blackfoot brothers. They found the Crow camp, took many scalps and plunder, and returned to Fort Benton to celebrate.

## Blackfoot Treaty

Unrest among the Indians on the Northern Plains forced government officials to bring the tribes together to arrange a settle-

*Left: Jerry Potts, Fort Benton trader and scout who became a legend with the North West Mounted Police as their guide and savior*

ment over land and hunting rights. In September 1865 many tribes of the Blackfoot Confederation and the Gros Ventres came to Fort Benton for negotiations and gifts. Translation of a forty-page document became so cumbersome that on the second day it was reduced to a few sentences. Late that afternoon a settlement was reached by all parties. The annuities took several days to disperse.

The treaty was accomplished by Acting Governor Thomas Francis Meagher and Indian Agent Gadson E. Upson. Old Bill Hamilton declared that Upson knew as much about an Indian as he did about the inhabitants of Jupiter. The treaty was short-lived. Open hostilities continued between the Indians and the whites for several more years.

## The Cannon and the Mule

Probably at the opening festivities during the late October treaty the famous cannon and mule legend occurred. Gladstone's diary noted that the last wagon train out of Cow Island that year carried an old four-pounder that was bound for Helena. An 1884 account in the River Press men-tions that a Diamond R freight train had arrived from Cow Island, was camped on the flats and had the barrel of a four-pounder strapped to the back of a mule. The stage was set.

Some thought it might be a good idea to show the Indians the strength of the "little gun" by discharging it while still strapped to the back of the mule. Most of the prominent men of the town were on hand, along with many chiefs from encampments surrounding the town.

Near the main entrance of the fort the mule was led to the bank of the river. With the muzzle pointing toward its tail and loaded with grape shot, an appointed officer, none other than X. Beidler, inserted a fuse and touched it off.

*Bottom: Far West, one of the gold rush boats that brought miners and freight to the Fort Benton levee in the 1860's; in 1876 under the command of Capt. Grant Marsh she carried wounded from the Little Big Horn to Bismarck.*

In a short time the stalwart mule heard the sizzling just back of his ears and turned his head to investigate. The *River Press* remarked about the next few minutes: "As his head turned, so his body turned and the howitzer began to take in other points of the compass. The mule became more excited as his curiosity became more and more intense. In a few seconds he either had his four feet in a bunch, making more revolutions a minute than the bystanders dared count and with the howitzer threatening destruction to everybody within a radius of a quarter of a mile, or he suddenly tried standing on his head with his heels and howitzer at a remarkable angle in the air."

The gathered circle of whites and Indians started to scatter. Col. Broadwater, Mose Solomon, H.A. Kennerly and Joe Healy dived over the river bank to a wet landing. Matt Carroll, George Steell and James Arnoux sprinted up the street and Hi Upham, Bill Hamilton and Johnny

Healy sought shelter on the ground. I.G. Baker and two of the peace commissioners headed for the fort. The Indians stood around wondering what all the excitement was about.

With a sudden puff of smoke the cannon discharged its grape shot toward the fort. According to the newspaper, the mule "with his heels in mid-air, was shaken with the most violent agitation . . . oh where was he? Ask of the wind, for no soul saw him. They will tell you a lonely, forlorn mule might have been seen turning over and over until he tumbled over the bank with the howitzer and cast anchor in the river." The shot hit the buffalo mural over the main gate. The paper reminded everyone that it been well perforated with shot, and with tongue in cheek stated it was X. Beidler's first buffalo. It was an exciting few minutes with no injuries, and left the Indians wondering about the antics of the Bentonites.

*Above:* X. Beidler: frequent visitor to Fort Benton, Vigilante, hangman and later U.S. Deputy Marshal

*Top left:* Steamboat Ida Rees tied up at the Fort Benton levee, where General Meagher fell from the steamer G.A. Thompson in 1867

*Above: Mary McDonald docked at the levee after a run from St. Louis during the gold rush*

*Below: I.G. Baker Home where Thomas Francis Meagher had his last supper, and where Fort Benton's first white child was born*

On the last day of the festivities the North Piegans got liquored up and rode through the river bottom with yards of calico tied to their horses' tails. They even threatened the Gros Ventres who were camped downriver from the fort. The Indians continued shouting and shooting throughout the night, up and down the streets of Fort Benton, "treeing" its small

population. Everyone stayed in their cellars for protection until the Indians left the next morning. At daybreak, the inhabitants reclaimed their town and everything returned to normal after most of the 5000 Indians had departed. This kind of affair was often referred to as "painting the town red" when blood was spattered on walls and board sidewalks after a night of hilarity and chaos.

## Governor Lost

General Thomas Francis Meagher first came to Fort Benton in 1864 as secretary to Sidney Edgerton, Montana's first territorial governor. Indian trouble brought him back to Fort Benton as the state's acting governor to negotiate the treaty, and later to collect guns and cannon for the

militia to fight an Indian war. Still hearing the drums and bugles of the Civil War, General Meagher, an Irish patriot and outlaw, dreamed of recapturing the glory of war in Montana.

Following his arrival in Fort Benton on July 1, 1867 Meagher dined with the I.G. Baker family, then retired to a cabin on the steamboat *G.A. Thompson* that was docked at the levee. Near midnight Meagher fell overboard and drowned; his body was never recovered. Rumors suggested many reasons for his death, but one must remember that Meagher was a

heavy drinker and that his death really may have been accidental.

# A Slight Misunderstanding

After all the trouble during the late 1860's, 1869 was no exception. In July two Garrison and Wyatt herders were killed north of Fort Benton by unidentified Indians. Without any investigation, the Blackfoot were blamed. (Later the culprits were found to be Crows.) A posse found a Blackfoot on the street who was promptly taken to the gallows. A second Indian was shot trying to leave town. According to W. S. Stocking, a large war party of Blackfoot seeking revenge rode into town, shooting and riding up and down the streets. Bentonites fought them in the streets, killing fifteen and chasing the rest out of town. That year there had been so many killings in Fort Benton that the Helena Herald hardly made mention of the encounter, simply noting that John

*Left: Governor Thomas Francis Meagher, Civil War hero and Irish patriot, drowned at the levee in Fort Benton in 1867.*

*Left: Sidewheeler Wm. J. Lewis was one of several boats to make it to Fort Benton during the gold rush that were not well adapted to upper river travel.*

Morgan and armed men drove Indians out of Fort Benton. It had been a bloody year for white and Indian alike.

By 1870 the placers were playing out and business had slowed in the river town. Steamboat arrivals declined to only a few each year. The next boom was about to begin with the opening of the Canadian West and five years of lawless whiskey trade. Fort Benton became the center of the whiskey trade and developed into the most important transportation center of the Northwest.

*Below: Steamer Viola Belle loading wood at a yard downriver; she was on her way to Fort Benton bringing gold seekers to the mountains.*

## The Parting Shot

As an end to this era of lawlessness, wild living and commercial growth, Winfield S. Stocking remarked, "Although it [Fort Benton] continued to be a mere village in size, in a commercial way it was Chicago of the Plains . . . It was the door through which all the gold hunters, adventurers, speculators, traders, land-seekers, big-game hunters, fugitives from justice, desperadoes and all the mean Indians then on the top of the earth entered the Northwest."

*Chapter 4*

# New Markets North

*With the placers playing out, Fort Benton businesses looked for the next Utopia and found one across the border in the Canadian West.*

## Opening New Markets

Hard rock mining was all that remained in the mountains by 1869. Many Front Street businesses closed and people moved on to the next bonanza.

Since 1670 western Canada had been owned and administered by the Hudson Bay Company, who had a virtual monopoly on all trade. In 1869 the Canadian government persuaded the Crown to return the Hudson Bay Company's holdings to Canada.

Called the North West Territories, the region opened to trade, creating new markets and land for Canadians. It was also ready for exploitation by all free traders from south of the border. They headed north from Fort Benton to capitalize on the whiskey trade for buffalo robes. With no law and order or government, big profits were made by trading with Indians north of the border. Not only did the free traders head north, but also company men backed by the big businesses of I.G. Baker and Co. and T.C. Power and Bro.

*Below:*
*Front Street was as empty as a ghost town in 1869. The placers were playing out, but Canadian trade was about to trigger the next boom.*

61

*Above: A.B. Hamilton gave his name to Fort Hamilton, unofficially called Fort Whoop-up.*

*Right: John J. Healy: trader, Indian agent, Sheriff of Choteau County and Hamilton's partner*

*Below: Fort Hamilton, the first and most notorious whiskey fort on the Oldman River*

# Whiskey Trade

Although most claimed to be free traders, many men were financed by and related to merchants in Fort Benton. Each season some traders switched companies for a better deal offered by a rival, and each season companies tried various schemes to put each other out of business. Profits were so great in the early years that even some owners, such as Charles Conrad and John D. Weatherwax, spent most of their time north of the border. They looked after company interests and kept a keen eye on the competition. The only

Huge profits were to be had with little overhead.

The founding of Fort Whoop-Up in 1869 signaled the beginning of an international, and illegal, liquor business unequaled anywhere. The whiskey trade lasted six years, with more violence than in many wars. Traders became rich, but Indians suffered social and mental degradation at the hands of both Americans and Canadians.

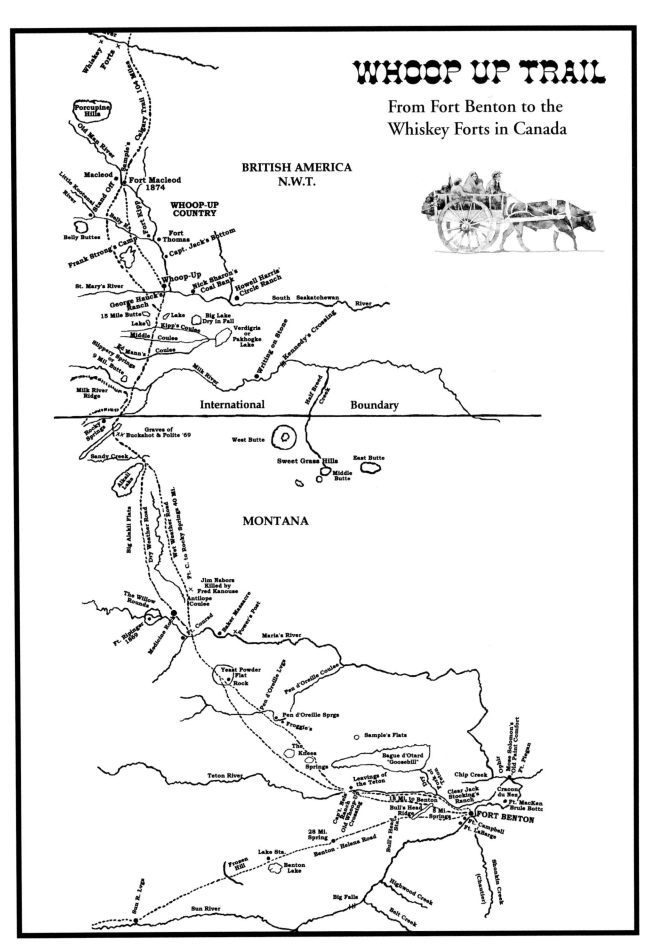

# WHOOP UP TRAIL

## From Fort Benton to the Whiskey Forts in Canada

Whiskey Forts ×

Calgary Trail 104 Mile

Porcupine Hills

Old Man River

Samples

**BRITISH AMERICA N.W.T.**

Macleod

Fort Macleod 1874

Little Kootenai River

Stand Off

Fort Kipp

**WHOOP-UP COUNTRY**

Belly River

Belly Buttes

Frank Strong's Camp

Fort Thomas

Capt. Jack's Bottom

St. Mary's River

Whoop-Up

Nick Sharon's Coal Bank

Howell Harris' Circle Ranch

George Hauck's Ranch

South Saskatchewan River

15 Mile Butte

Lake

Lake

Kipp's Coulee

Big Lake Dry in Fall

Verdigris or Pakhogke Lake

Middle Coulee

Ed Mann's Coulee

Kennedy's Crossing

Slippery Springs or 9 Mil. Butte

Milk River

Writing on Stone

Milk River Ridge

Half Breed Creek

**International          Boundary**

Rocky Springs

Graves of Buckshot & Polite '69

West Butte

Sandy Creek

Alkali Lake

Sweet Grass Hills

East Butte

Middle Butte

Big Alkali Flats

Dry Weather Road

Wet Weather Road 40 Mi.

Ft. C. to Rocky Springs 40 Mi.

**MONTANA**

Jim Nabors Killed by Fred Kanouse

Antelope Coulee

The Willow Rounds

Ft. Bichner 1869

Medicine Rock

Conrad

Baker Massacre

Power's Post

Maria's River

Yeast Powder Flat Rock

Pen d'Oreille Lvgs

Pen d'Oreille Coulee

Pen d'Oreille Sprgs

Froggie's

Sample's Flats

The Knees

Bague d'Otard "Goosebill"

Springs

Teton River

Leavings of the Teton

Ft. of Ford

Ophir

Mose Solomon's Old Paint Comfort

Ft. Piegan

Chip Creek

Cracon du Nez

Ft. MacKen Brule Bottc

Capt. Nels Ranch Old Ranch Whoop-Up Crossing

15 Mi. to Benton

Clear Jack Stocking's Ranch

Bull's Head Ridge

8 Mi. Springs

**FORT BENTON**

Bull's Head Butte

Ft. Campbell

Ft. LaBarge

28 Mi. Spring

Lake Sta.

Benton - Helena Road

Shonkin Creek (Chantier)

Frozen Hill

Benton Lake

Sun R. Lvgs

Sun River

Big Falls

Highwood Creek

Belt Creek

# Whiskey Post

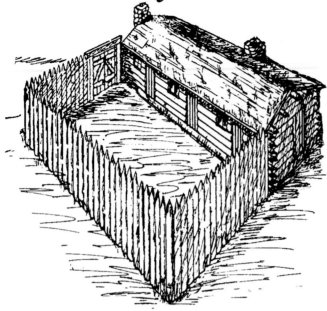

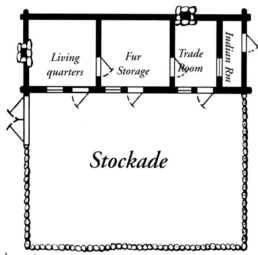

Living quarters | Fur Storage | Trade Room | Indian Rm

### Stockade

*Above:* Typical layout of a Canadian trading post during the whiskey trade

danger faced by traders was straying too far from the trading post; they might lose their hair to some drunken Indian who had been robbed of his robes.

Indian whiskey was cheap; it was watered down and seasoned with peppers and gun powder. Thirteen gallons of "high wine" as it was called could make up to two hundred gallons of rot-gut Indian whiskey. With little expense invested in trade goods, large profits resulted for free traders, company men and Fort Benton's merchant princes.

## Whoop-Up

Johnny Healy, Indian agent and trader, and I.G. Baker's nephew A.B. Hamilton headed across the border with casks of illegal whiskey and trade goods provided by the Baker firm. They built Fort Whoop-Up on the Oldman River and realized a profit of $40,000 after the first season. Their fort was the most noted whiskey fort, the infamous symbol of the whiskey trade north of the

*Right:* Bull team headed north supplying trade goods, rifles, blankets and of course, whiskey by the barrel

border. Over forty whiskey posts were built as far north as Edmonton and the Great Slave Lake.

Both Baker and Power firms hurried to establish trade stores from the Cypress Hills to the western mountains. In 1871 the Conrads sent Howell Harris north to build Fort Conrad and Fort Standoff the next season. When the whiskey days were over, Harris became a respected cattleman running the Circle brand herd of the Conrad brothers in Canada.

At a whiskey fort, trade occurred through a wicket (a small opening in the wall) with the Indians outside of the fort. The trader usually had a tub full of Indian whiskey beside him. When an Indian pushed a buffalo robe through the opening, the trader handed back a tin cup of the concoction which was promptly swallowed! A horse traded for a quart of fire water. Within a few hours of the beginning of trade, the area

*Top: Malcolm Clarke was factor at Fort Benton and later a rancher on the Little Prickly Pear, where he was killed by his Blackfoot relatives. His murder started the last Blackfoot War that ended with the Baker Massacre in 1870.*

*Bottom: Located at the mouth of the Judith River, Camp Cooke was the first military post in Montana. It was inhabited from 1866 to 1869, when rats not Indians drove out the military.*

surrounding the post was full of drunken Indians; shooting and shouting went on all night. Traders watched the party from the security of their fort, and mixed up more fire water for the next day's business. Their recipe was to add one quart of rot-gut whiskey, hot peppers, a touch of gun powder, chewing tobacco, and some black molasses to river water, and simmer until strong enough to burn all the way down.

## Traders and Trouble

As in any lawless land, greed nurtured violence and confrontation among the traders. At Fort Spitzee a group of wolfers was organized for Baker interests into the Spitzee Cavalry by the infamous Johnny Evans. The group's ostensible purpose was to prevent the trade of repeating rifles to the Indians, but their real mission was to thwart Power business in Canada. Johnny Healy, then working for Power at Fort Whoop-Up, refused to succumb to the cavalry's demands and the conflict was settled with words rather than guns. It should be noted, however, that a loaded cannon was hidden

in the trade store! Minor incidents occurred throughout those lawless years, encouraged by both rival companies in an effort to gain more of the whiskey trade. Confrontations continued until 1881 when they divided the Canadian trade.

After Hamilton and Healy returned to Montana, Donald Watson Davis, Baker's chief trader took over at Fort Whoop-Up. He was in charge when the Mounties arrived and was instrumental in establishing the legitimacy of the I.G. Baker Company's trade in Canada. Davis later managed Baker businesses at Fort Macleod until the company sold their Canadian interests to the Hudson Bay Company in 1890. He served in the Canadian Parliament, remaining in Canada the rest of his life.

## Indians and the Metis

Just two years into Dominion status, the Canadian government had its hands full. In Manitoba the Metis, under Louis Riel, wanted independence. The rebellion was put down and Riel came to Montana in exile. With sympathy and encouragement from the Fenian Movement under Irish lawyer John J. Donnelly, Riel

was urged to continue the rebellion. After several years in Fort Benton, Lewistown, St. Peter's Mission and Carroll, Riel returned to Canada in 1885 to lead a second rebellion. In Regina he received a noose as his reward for treason, ending the second Metis rebellion and crushing the hopes of Fenians in Montana.

In 1869 Mountain Chief's son was killed on Front Street; his body was unceremoniously dumped into the well in the HooDoo Block. There was more unrest in Fort Benton and on the trails out of town. Malcolm Clarke, an ex-Fort Benton trader,

*Above:* *Lt. James H. Bradley, Montana's first historian, wrote of his experiences in the Indian Campaign of 1876.*

was murdered at Sieben by his Blackfoot relatives. An all-night shoot-out occurred in Fort Benton when the Indians charged wildly up and down the streets. Frightened citizens again hid in their cellars until morning when the Indians rode out of town.

## A Military Post

The War Department closed Camp Cooke in July 1869 due to desertion, isolation, the great distances to population centers . . . and rats. In November Company B of the 13th Infantry moved to Fort Benton where they established a military reservation. Fort Benton became a military post charged with protecting the river port from the Indians and receiving and forwarding freight to Fort Shaw and Fort Ellis. With arrival of the military, a telegraph line was built between Fort Benton and Fort Shaw connecting it with the capital in Helena.

After establishment of the military post, there was no Indian trouble in Fort Benton. The biggest military disaster occurred on December 17, 1872 when a unit of seventy-five men traveling between Fort Benton and Fort Shaw were caught in a blizzard; the Montana winter claimed forty who died from exposure. During a winter campaign against marauding Indians, the military attacked Heavy Runner's peaceful Blackfoot

*Left: Military encampment of tents, wagons and horses at Fort Benton. The fort was used as a bivouac for troops who were transported on the Missouri River.*

band on the Marias. The massacre of a Piegan village by the U.S. Army under the command of Major Baker brought an end to hostilities in 1870. The Baker Massacre and the dreaded smallpox ended forever the threat of the "terrible" Blackfoot in Montana.

While in residence at the fort, the military constructed a new headquarters of adobe bricks scavenged from other dilapidated fort structures. They also built a stable of hand-cut lumber from the mountains that housed fifty-six mounts, a laundry and quarters for the laundresses. One of the lieutenants stationed at the fort was James H. Bradley, recognized as Montana's first historian.

By 1874 the fort's buildings were uninhabitable. Officers and men were quartered in town, many in the Choteau House Hotel. The fort was used only for drills, stables, laundry and storage. When the military left in 1881, the land and buildings of the old fort were claimed by Francis H. Eastman to whom they had been deeded by the Northwest Fur Company in 1877.

## Cypress Hills Massacre

After five years of whiskey-running across the border, the illicit commerce came to a sudden end. Continued rivalry between the Power and Baker firms touched off a conflict in the Cypress Hills. In June 1873 a group of Fort Benton's "finest" was headed home when their horses were stolen on the Marias. They rallied immediately back in Fort Benton under the leadership of Johnny Evans and headed north, mainly looking for a fight and maybe for the thieves.

In the Cypress Hills the marauders liquored up at Farwell's Post and at Mose Solomon's, the notorious owner of the Medicine Lodge Saloon in Fort Benton. The next day they attacked an Assiniboine camp and about twenty Indians were killed. Only one white man was lost; Ed Grace was buried under the floor at Farwell's Post.

With the Cypress Hills Massacre the Hudson Bay Company had just cause to bring the North West Mounted Police to the

**Above:** *Wagons ready to leave Fort Benton for the Canadian whiskey forts*

**Above right:** *Seal of the Hudson Bay Co.; according to the opposition, HBC stood for "Here Before Christ."*

**Far right:** *NWMP in original 1873 uniform: pill box hat, tan pants, scarlet tunic and brown boots*

northern prairies the next year. The company was not particularly interested in the welfare of the Indians, but the Americans were cutting deeply into their trade with whiskey sales. With arrival of the Mounties, illegal business north of the border ceased nearly overnight. Established companies and free traders alike swept away all signs of the whiskey trade and were almost respectable by the next day. No one claimed any knowledge of the six years of cheap whiskey, high profits and destruction of the Indian culture.

**Right:** *Inside Fort Hamilton (Whoop-Up), the most infamous whiskey fort, located near Lethbridge, Alberta*

*Chapter 5*

# Redcoats and Respectability

*Never before had so few brought law and order to such a vast and hostile land, and still maintained the respect of its native people.*

## Influence on Both Sides of the Border

The presence of the Mounties brought the "toughest town in the West" into a new era of respectability. Law came because business demanded it. At an end were the days of frequent murders, a cavalry troop for security when Federal warrants were served, and marshals and government officials bootlegging whiskey in Canada.

With insistent prodding from the Hudson Bay Company, the Canadian government in Ottawa finally responded. The North West Mounted Police were organized in 1873. Recruitment had hardly begun when the story of the Cypress Hills Massacre hit Eastern newspapers.

The Mounties received their orders to march West in all haste, and bring law and order to an un-civilized land overrun with whiskey traders from Fort Benton. The police force was charged with stopping the whiskey traffic, patrolling the bor-der, collecting customs and curbing any Fenian invasion from the rogue

Irish in Montana. In 1874 the thin scarlet line came West; by September they were lost and starving in Whoop-Up country. There was little grass and rations were running low when an early snow blanketed the vast northern plains.

## Lost in the Wilderness

Led by Colonel Macleod, a party of Mounties went to Fort Benton for help. Upon their arrival, the whiskey traders realized that their illicit activities were over. From the Conrad brothers Macleod obtained knowledge of the country to the north and purchased supplies from their I.G. Baker stores. A bull team headed for the Three Buttes (Sweet Grass Hills) to resupply the police force.

Col. Macleod requested a guide who knew the country around the Oldman River; Charles Conrad introduced him to Jerry Potts who was hired immediately. A legend was in the

***Below:*** *Mountie in scarlet tunic and white pith helmet*

71

*Above: Col. Macleod (second from right) and three other police officers during the first years of duty in the West*

*Above: Freight wagons on Main Street in Fort Benton headed north to Fort Macleod. The Benton Record building is in the background on Baker Street.*

*Bottom: Fort Macleod, first post of the North West Mounted Police, was built in 1874 in the heart of Canada's whiskey fort country.*

## The End of an Era

Traders poured out their Indian whiskey and quietly returned to Montana; Fort Whoop-Up was taken over by the Mounties without a shot. News spread across Whoop-Up country that the party was over. In one fell swoop those few men in scarlet tunics brought law and order not only to the Canadian West but also to the Montana frontier.

Fort Benton, the most lawless town in the West, drastically changed character and the whiskey trade was history. Legitimate trade began with Canada. A few, like J.D. Weatherwax, learned the hard way; they were arrested, their goods were seized and they served time in jail.

## A Few Years Left

In 1872 the Northern Pacific Railroad arrived in Bismarck, North Dakota, but the financial panic of 1873 stopped all rail building for several years. There were fifteen years of trade between the railhead in Bismarck and Fort Benton. Steamboats brought freight to Fort Benton where it was loaded onto bull trains and hauled up the Whoop-Up Trail. It was eventually sold in the Canadian stores of Fort Benton's merchant princes.

The Hudson Bay Company's troubles were not over yet. Fort Benton merchants shipped goods from the East by rail, brought them to Fort Benton by steamboat,

making. Potts not only knew the country, but was also an accomplished frontiersman. He led them to the Oldman River and helped construct Fort Macleod. Potts became a hero to the Force, a steadying influence for those inexperienced Eastern troopers who taught them survival on the western frontier.

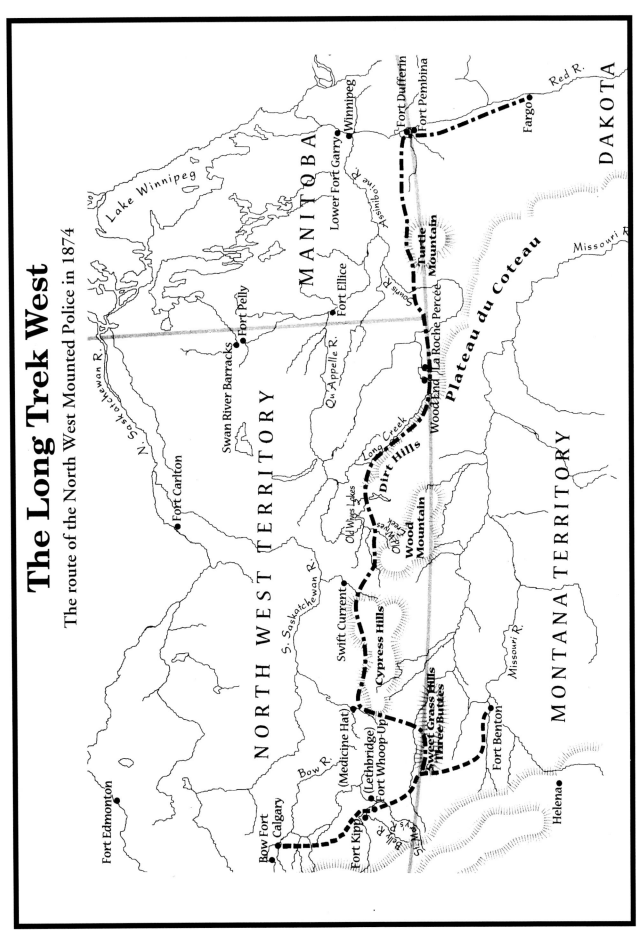

# The Long Trek West

The route of the North West Mounted Police in 1874

then hauled the merchandise overland on the Whoop-Up Trail. Their expense was far less than Canadian merchants who shipped their goods across the Canadian prairies. Government contracts to supply the Indians and the North West Mounted Police were secured by the Baker and Power firms in Fort Benton, who underbid the Hudson Bay Company year after year.

*Top: Fort Benton levee at the height of the freighting season. In busy years some freight was not moved to its destination until November.*

*Right: William Wesley Van Orsdel, 1848 - 1919. "Brother Van," a Methodist preacher, was a legend in the West and the founding father of the Methodist Church in Montana.*

## Brother Van

On June 30, 1872 the steamer *Far West* docked at the Fort Benton levee. Down the gangplank walked a man who made a tremendous impact on the religious lives of Montanans and Blackfoot alike. Then just twenty-four years old, William Wesley Van

*Right: Steamboats on the Bismarck levee load for the upriver trip to Fort Benton. Steamboat Western next to bank, E.H. Dufree along side and Nellie Peck in the rear. All belonged to the Peck Line that served the upper river.*

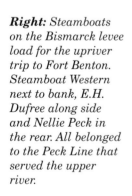

Orsdel, a Methodist evangelist, became a Montana legend. According to the stories, he held his first service in a saloon on Front Street after convincing the bartender to close down until he had finished. His first message was well received in that boisterous river front saloon after his famous rendition of "Diamonds in the Rough."

"Brother Van" was a friend of saint and sinner alike throughout his years of riding the circuit on the Montana frontier. His ministry to the Blackfoot was special; the Indians knew him as "Great Heart." In later years his birthday party was held annually in Fort Benton. Shortly after the celebration in 1919, Brother Van passed on at the age of 71. His Blackfoot friends remarked sadly that they now had one friend in heaven.

## Big Business and The Last of the Indian Wars

Baker and Power businesses grew. In a cooperative venture they established the Benton Packet Co. (the Block P steamboat line) on the Missouri in 1875. Large freight outfits owned by Baker, Power and other Bentonites moved goods from Fort

*Top: T.C. Power and Bro.'s first store on Front Street. In 1867 Power opened for business in Fort Benton in a tent loaned by I.G. Baker.*

*Bottom: Baker's first store, where the great commercial empire began in 1866*

# Baker Empire in Fort Benton

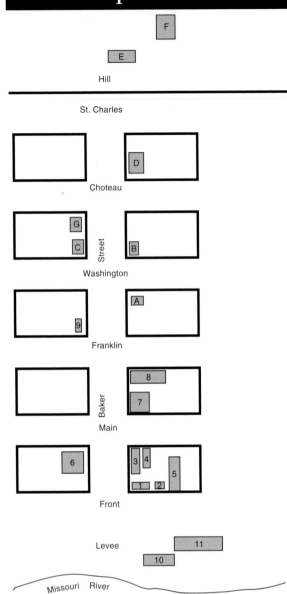

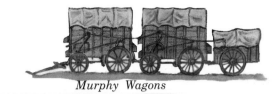

*Murphy Wagons*

## Business Buildings

1. Original Store
2. First House
3. Original Warehouse
4. Bonded Warehouse (Canadian Trade)
5. Thwing House (Hotel)
6. Second Brick Store and Warehouse
7. Benton Record Bldg. (Newspaper & Bank)
8. Park Stables
9. Blacksmith Shop
10. Levee Warehouse I
11. Levee Warehouse II

## Homes

A. C.E. Conrad Bungalow
B. Joseph H. Conrad
C. Joseph A. Baker and Anna M. Conrad
D. W.G. Conrad Mansion
E. James W. Conrad (father and mother)
F. C.W. Price and Mollie Conrad
G. T.J. Todd and Mattie Conrad

# The Family

*Front, l to r: W.G. Conrad, T.J. Todd, C.W. Price*
*Rear, l to r: C.E. Conrad, I.G. Baker, Dr. D.E.*
*Adams*
*Todd, Price and Adams married Conrad sisters.*

Benton to northern points. Freighting outfits took from fourteen to twenty days, traveling at ten to fifteen miles a day, to make the trip North.

Fort Benton continued to prosper during the last of the Indian wars. In 1876 the Sioux and Cheyenne ambushed Custer on the Little Big Horn. Young Lieutenant James Bradley was with the Montana Column that tended the dead and wounded, and sent them down the Yellowstone on board the steamboat *Far West*. Sitting Bull moved north of the border, prompting the presence of troops in northern Montana for several years.

Fort Benton's first newspaper, the *Benton Record,* was founded in 1875. In May it reported, "Benton is all business just now. The river is hid by a wall of freight . . . "

The Nez Perce left their Idaho home in 1877 and began the trek across Montana. They won a series of pitched battles with the army, staying just out of reach as they headed for the Canadian border and protection from the Queen Mother. Colonel Gibbon and the Montana Column were again called into service. At the Battle of the Big Hole Lieutenant Bradley was killed instantly.

In October the Nez Perce were headed north to a river

*Above: Thomas C. Power, Fort Benton merchant prince who later was a U.S. Senator from Montana*

*Above left: John W. Power, Thomas' younger brother, ran the Fort Benton operation.*

*Bottom: Baker Street homes of the Family. William G. Conrad's mansion is at the end of the street. His brother John owned the next house down the street on the right. Across the street from John's home is the honeymoon cottage of Charles E. Conrad and his new bride Alicia. The last two homes belonged to merchants associated with the I.G. Baker Co.*

77

# Commercial Establishments of Baker and Power During the Canadian Trade

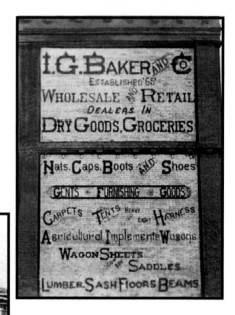

**Above:** *Power's second store, built in 1879 at the height of Canadian trade*

**Left:** *Baker's first store in Fort Macleod*

**Left:** *Baker warehouses on Fort Benton's Main Street*

**Above:** *I.G. Baker's second store on Main Street, built in 1878; the first store became T.J. Todd's liquor business. Todd was the Conrad's brother-in-law.*

**Left:** *Beautiful stone I.G. Baker Co. store in Calgary. Baker enterprises rivaled the Hudson Bay Co. for trade until the Canadian Pacific Railroad arrived.*

*Top*: Main Street of Fort Macleod. The largest building on the street is the I.G. Baker Co. store in the center.

crossing at Cow Island. There were still piles of private and government freight at the Landing, left by the steamboats during low water. Major Guido Ilges organized a force of fifty volunteers. With Company F of the 7th Infantry they went downriver from Fort Benton to intercept the Indians and help protect the freight at Cow Island Landing.

When the Nez Perce crossed the Missouri at the Landing, their request for supplies was denied. They pinned down the army overnight in their rifle pits, took what supplies they needed and burned the rest. The Fort Benton volunteers did not arrive until the next morning. After a pitched battle up Cow Creek, they decided caution was the best part of valor and returned to the Landing to await reinforcements. The Nez Perce headed on north. They were confronted several days later on Snake Creek in the Bear's Paw Mountains, and forced to surrender to the U.S. Army under Gen. O.O. Howard and Col. Nelson Miles.

One of the volunteers, John W. Tattan, was saved from certain death by his brass US belt buckle. A retired Civil War veteran, Tattan was serving as U.S. District Judge in Fort Benton. He brought Chief Joseph's surrender rifle back to Fort Benton, which had been given to him by General Howard. Gen. Howard admonished Tattan, the only U.S. government official in the region, to always keep this rifle in Montana.

*Above*: Maj. Guido Ilges, commander of Company F of the 7th Infantry stationed at Fort Benton

*Left*: Chief Joseph surrendered for the Nez Perce at the Battle of the Bear's Paw.

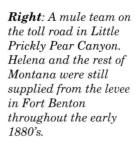

*Right*: A mule team on the toll road in Little Prickly Pear Canyon. Helena and the rest of Montana were still supplied from the levee in Fort Benton throughout the early 1880's.

79

*Right: Gen. O.O. Howard, Commanding General at the Battle of the Bear's Paw in October 1877, who had chased the Nez Perce from Idaho clear across Montana*

*Far right: Col. Nelson Miles was able to catch the Nez Perce before they crossed into Canada. He later became a general and one of the most successful Indian fighters in the U.S. Army.*

*Below: Fort Walsh, the North West Mounted Police post in the Cypress Hills, was in the region served by T.C. Power and Bro. during the 1880's.*

## Business As Usual

After the 1877 campaign, life settled down. Fort Benton had grown into one of Montana's three most important cities, and enjoyed a few more great years as the transportation center of the Northwest. The wood and log shanties of the 1860's were replaced with buildings of locally-manufactured brick. The first brick building was the school, constructed in 1877. The next year Baker and Power put up new brick stores and ware-

houses to handle the Canadian trade.

Steamboat arrivals reached a new peak and the levee was piled high with freight. The last three years of the 1870's were boom years on the river. Twenty-five to thirty percent of the freight was shipped up the Whoop-Up. Until railroads cut across the prairies of Alberta and Montana, steamboats reigned supreme. In 1877 twenty-five steamboats tied up to the levee. During the great boom of 1878, steamboat traffic jumped to 49 arrivals with over 20 million pounds of freight. The building boom was on and Fort Benton's population skyrocketed.

Overloaded wagons creaked

up the Whoop-Up Trail to Calgary, Lethbridge, and Edmonton. Buffalo robes flowed out of Canada during those years at about 50,000 annually and were shipped by steamer to Eastern markets. Even during the low water year of 1879 shipping was nearly as great as the previous year. There were 42 landings, again with over 20 million pounds of freight.

During those years the cost of freight was equal to the price of the goods. Steamboating and

*Above:* N.W.M.P. detachment at Ten Mile in 1886 south of Fort Walsh on the Benton Road. Notice the variety of uniforms.

*Below:* Steamboat Helena of the Block P Line, one of T.C. Power's fast packets on the Upper Missouri during the Canadian trade

*Above: Bull team from Fort Macleod loaded with wood and coal from Lethbridge. Goods needed in Fort Benton created a two-way pay load for bullwhackers and more money for the companies.*

*Below: A small Mountie post with whitewashed log cabins in the Cypress Hills*

freighting were very lucrative businesses, and two of Fort Benton's mercant princes were active in both activities. After years of rivalry in the Canadian trade, in 1881 Baker and Power agreed to divide the contracts and the Canadian trade. Baker trade interests were along the mountains to the west, Power had the Cypress Hills and the eastern prairies. One firm would bid high, the other low so there was no competition for the Canadian contracts. A portion of each contract was kicked back to the other firm; there was plenty for both to prosper.

The boom lasted until the mid-1880's. To the east ties and rails were laid and spikes were driven by gangs of Irish, Chinese and other immigrants. The end of the steamboat era was at hand. No longer would the way west be up the mighty Missouri from St. Louis to Fort Benton, but across rails of steel. Fort Benton's role in Montana history and in the history of the Northwest was nearing an end.

## A Last Hoorah to the Whiskey Trade

James Willard Schultz made a poignant comment about the whiskey trade: "I make no excuse for the whiskey trade. It was wrong, and none realized it better than we when we were dispensing the stuff. It caused untold suffering, many deaths, great demoralization among these people of the plains. There was but one redeeming feature about it: The trade was at a time when it did not deprive them of the necessities of life; there was always more meat, more fur to be had for the killing of it. In comparison with various Government officials and rings who robbed and starved the Indians to death on the reservation after the buffalo disappeared, we were saints."

*Chapter 6*

# Seven Golden Years

*Since 1860 Fort Benton had been the head of navigation on the river, but for a few short years it was also the transportation center of the Northwest and Montana's most strategic city.*

## Fire at the Courthouse

*"The courthouse was blazing. Red flames were bursting from several of its rear windows . . . Came running a file of men drawing the fire engine, and another crew hauling the hose cart. Tom Todd firemanhatted stood upon the engine shouting orders. One end of the hose was attached to the engine the suction end reeled out to I know not what water hole. As the nozzled hose was snaked onto the building, a dozen men grasp each long hand rail of the engine and the pumping began - click, clack, click, clack . . .*

*All soon realized that the courthouse was doomed, that our puny efforts could not save it so we dispersed and let it burn . . . repaired to Keno Bill's saloon to quench our thirst. Said one, as we lined before the bar:*

*"Strange how the courthouse got afire, Surely its stoves are not kept going these hot days."*

*"Huh. Nothin' strange about it." replied Keno Bill. "Some records in it just nat'rally had to be*

*Left: Left at Cow Island over the winter, Fort Benton's first fire engine finally arrived in 1882.*

*destroyed to keep certain fellers I know out of a heap of trouble."*

The account from James Willard Schultz 's <u>Blackfeet and Buffalo</u> entitled *"Fire at Fort Benton Courthouse"* best explains the transition from a tough town to a cultured city in the 1880's. With the courthouse in flames, the official past was lost forever. The

*Left: The new courthouse in 1884; fire destroyed the wooden one on Main Street.*

*Above: Hose Cart Company No. 1 on the 4th of July 1884. It was one of three volunteer fire companies organized in the 1880's.*

*Below: Fort Benton in 1878 at the beginning of the building boom. The steamer Benton is tied to the upper levee.*

town became civilized with that single stroke of a match, well almost.

## Civilization

By 1878 the building boom was underway. River trade reached its zenith with the arrival of sixty boats. It was the last big year of the robe trade; 20,000 were sent downriver.

The Benton Packet Co. controlled the river from Benton to Bismarck, the western terminus of the Northern Pacific. No one could imagine that in a very few years it would all be over.

*Left: Fort Benton's first real schoolhouse; built in 1877, it was the town's first brick building.*

From 1878 to 1884 all brick buildings in Fort Benton were constructed by three contractors: Tweedy & Combs, Gus Senieur and John Wilton. The greatest effort was in 1882 when three million bricks were laid, $200,000 worth of buildings.

## End of Trade

1875 was the final chapter of the whiskey trade. In connection with the Cypress Hills affair, the Canadian government attempted to extradite some of Fort Benton's businessmen for trial in Canada. Warrants were sent out by the Federal government, to be served

*Left below: Billy Rowe: stage driver, trader and Chouteau County Sheriff*

*Below: The new jail built in 1881 was thought to be too fancy by the public; it cost Sheriff John J. Healy the next election.*

*Right: Park Livery on Baker Street, one of the company's many enterprises. Young Frank Flanagan is on horseback.*

*Above: John J. Donnelly: Irish patriot, Fenian General, and Speaker of the Territorial House of Representatives*

*Below: Baker Street with the Benton Record Building and warehouses of the I.G. Baker Co.*

by Deputy U.S. Marshals X. Biedler and Charles Hard. They were met in Fort Benton at gun point and chased out of town. The marshals returned the next time with a troop of U.S. Cavalry from Fort Shaw and the warrants were served. With the eloquent tongue of Irishman John J. Donnelly at their defense, the businessmen were found innocent at their trial in Helena.

Their acquittal showed that the city fathers still had plenty of political clout, and sometimes firearms, to save the day. In glee Johnny Evans came home and renamed his Front Street saloon . . . The Extradition.

Donnelly, one of many Fenians in Fort Benton who hated the king, had participated in three unsuccessful invasions of Canada and was a Civil War veteran of the Union Army. He was also the leader of the volunteers who went to Cow Island in 1877 to fight the Nez Perce. Donnelly was elected Speaker of the Territorial Legislature. In an act of despondency he committed suicide after the Metis Rebellion failed.

*Left: Grand Union Hotel, Victorian magnificence shortly after her grand opening in 1882*

# First Brick Buildings

The building boom continued until 1883. The Conrads built a two-story warehouse and store on the corner of Baker and Main. Across the street they also erected the three-story mansard-roofed Benton Record Building that housed Fort Benton's first newspaper and two banks. After a fabled career as Indian agent, whiskey trader, prospector and farmer, Johnny Healy was appointed Chouteau County Sheriff in 1877. The next year he became editor of the *Benton Record.* In 1882 Healy lost the election to Billy Rowe; voters felt the new brick jail was far too luxurious for common criminals. By 1885 he was on his way to Alaska and a new gold frontier in the Klondike.

With business establishments near the river and homes toward the hill, the commercial

*Left: Charles and Alicia Conrad with St. Paul's Sunday School class at their wedding cottage in 1885*

giant I.G. Baker and Company owned almost the entire five-block length of Baker Street. Most were built of brick during the boom period.

Under the leadership of the Conrad brothers, the I. G. Baker Company not only became the biggest business in town, but also the largest mercantile business in Montana. Its far-flung empire stretched from the Great Slave Lake and Edmonton in the north to New Orleans, New York and Montreal in the south and east. Company headquarters were in the two transportation centers of the West, St. Louis and Fort Benton. The giant enterprise monopolized trade in the Northwest and did millions in foreign trade as far away as London and St. Petersburg.

*Above: Chouteau County Courthouse is the second oldest in Montana and is still serving the county government.*

*Inset: Gus Senieur, builder of the courthouse and many other brick structures during the building boom of 1878-1884*

*Right: Flanagan's Drugstore, an adobe framed building. The famous bell Michael was given to the Church of the Immaculate Conception by Michael Flanagan.*

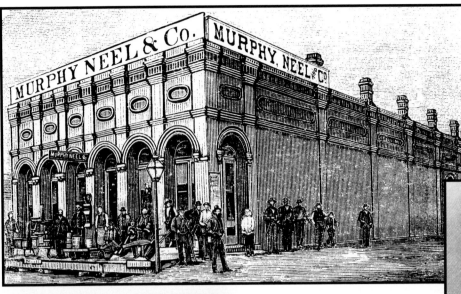

*Left: Murphy-Neel Co., an uptown business with W.S. Wetzel Co. and Kleinschmidt Bros.*

*Right: John T. Murphy: merchant, freighter and cattleman*

*Left: Hans J. Wackerlin: tinsmith and hardware partner with T.C. Power. Wackerlin came to Montana on the steamer Richmond with Quantrill*

*Below: Wackerlin Hardware and Choteau House on Front Street in the 1890's. The army still bivouacked at the old fort during summer.*

GRAND UNION HOTEL

SPITZLEY & TRAVERS
PROPRIETORS
FORT BENTON, M.T.

*Above: Interior of the bar in the 1880's, a gathering place for area cattlemen and sheepmen*

# Grand Union Hotel
## Queen on the Riverside

*Above: The cowboy was shot by the night clerk for trying to ride his horse up the main stairway.*

*Inset: Tom J. Todd, owner 1880's-1890's*

*Above: Lobby and main stairway with Mr. and Mrs. Charles Lepley, owners from 1917 to 1952*

*Right: Dining room in the 1880's with white linen, cut glass and silver service*

90

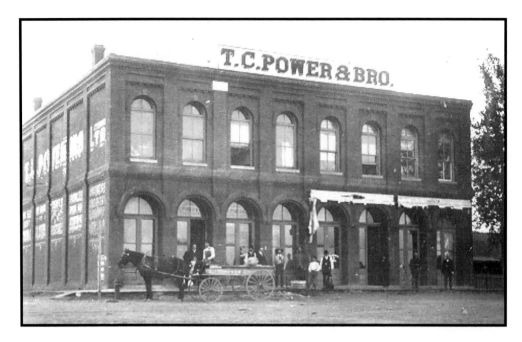

*Left:* T.C. Power's new brick store on Front Street was built to rival Baker's that had been completed on Main Street.

Charles Conrad returned from Canada with his half-breed son and married Alicia Stanford, the sister of a Mountie. They moved into their new two-story brick bungalow where they lived until the firm went out of business in 1893. Charles and Alicia moved to the Flathead Valley and built a beautiful mansion with money garnered from the Canadian trade.

In 1879 T.C. Power and Bro. constructed a two-story brick structure across the street from their first store. They built brick additions as their commercial interests expanded in Montana and Canada.

## Victorian Grandeur

The two largest brick structures erected in Fort Benton were the Grand Union Hotel and the Chouteau County Courthouse. The Grand Union, built by a group of businessmen in 1882, was said to be the finest establishment between St. Paul and the Pacific coast. The three-story hotel sits on the banks of the Missouri; its

extensive corbelling, wrought iron balconies and ornate chimneys were an impressive sight, whether one came to Fort Benton by boat or by road. Furnished with Victorian appointments, the dining room's silver service, white linen and Bavarian china served the rich and famous. There was a ladies parlor on the second floor with a private stairway to the dining room, so the ladies were not exposed to the rowdy crowd in the saloon or lobby.

*Bottom:* Billy Rowe and his brother Charlie operated the Benton-Helena Stage Co. in the 1880's. Hang on for your life, Charlie was at a full gallop with a six-horse hitch!

91

*Above:* Block P trademark of T.C. Power and Bro. Ltd.

*Above:* Benton Record Building housed Fort Benton's first newspaper, two banks and I.G. Baker Co. offices.

Rooms on the third floor were smaller and less opulent. A guest had to walk downstairs to use the two-story privy out back! Saddle rooms and sample rooms accommodated salesmen; in the back of the bar was a poker room where cattle spreads sometimes exchanged ownership with the turn of a card. All in all, it was a grand place that enjoyed three or four years of

splendor before the end of the steamboat era.

The Chouteau County Courthouse was built of brick in 1884 after the wood-frame structure burned in January 1883. Constructed next to the new brick jail, the imposing structure symbolized the prominence and wealth of Fort Benton and Chouteau County. The clock tower with its weathervane made the courthouse the tallest structure in town. Its classical design was from Kees and Fisk of Minneapolis; the contractor was Gus Senieur. The building was the last important structure constructed of local brick.

*Right:* A member of Fort Benton's Chinese community working in the garden. Across Front Street is the Gans and Klein clothing store and the Stockmen's National Bank.

## *Menu*

## *Menu*

*Platt's Select Raw*

Puree of Chicken.        Mock Turtle.

Baked Salmon Tomato Sauce.
Potato Croquettes.

Salmi of Prairie Chicken.
Sweet Breads Larded with French Peas
Chicken Liver Omelettes.
Pine Apple Fritters.

→UNCLE ✳ TOBY ✳ PUNCH←

Sirloin of Beef with Brown Gravy
Roast Sucking Pig with Bread Dressing
Apple Sauce.

Roast Young Turkey Cranberry Sauce
Saddle of Venison ✳ Haunch of Elk
With Currant Jelly.

## *Menu*

Chicken Salad.        Shrimp Salad.

Dressed Celery.

Cold Corned Beef        Ham.

Mashed Potatoes.        Garden Peas.
Sweet Corn on Cob.
Hot Slaw.

Mince Pies.        Lemon Cream Pies.
Cranberry Pies.
English Plum Pudding ✳ Rum Sauce

Assorted Cake.   Confectionery.
Vanilla Ice Cream.

Fruit.    Nuts.

Edam Cheese.        Coffee

---

On the second floor of the courthouse is a large courtroom furnished with an impressive raised judge's bench and high-backed chairs for the jury. The last death sentence was imposed in 1913 and the accused was hanged on the courthouse lawn. The event was attended by invitation only to selected citizens of Chouteau County.

## New-Found Society

In the few years between 1878 and 1884, Fort Benton was a city of wealth and high society. A beautiful white fire engine came upriver to a new brick firehouse, staffed by the Volunteer Fire Department of four companies. The Firemen's Ball at the Grand Union was the year's social event, ranking right up there with Christmas Eve at the Grand Union.

The holiday dinner menu rivaled that of the Waldorf. A huge Christmas tree in the center of the dining room, the halls decked out with boughs of holly and women in their floor-length gowns swirling to orchestra music made it a night to remember.

*Above: 1880's Bill of Fare for Christmas Eve dinner in the dining room of the Grand Union*

*Left: Little Bacchus, Roman god of pleasure, from the cover of the Christmas Eve menu*

# Fort Benton Homes of the 1880's

*Top:* Merchant W.S. Wetzel's home, later owned by banker C.E. Duer

*Above:* Judge Tattan's home built in 1878 with Mrs. Tattan in front

*Inset:* Judge John H. Tattan, first U.S. District Judge in northern Montana and hero of the Nez Perce fight at Cow Island

*Above:* Charles E. Duer, banker and cattleman

*Above:* W.G. Conrad's mansion; Conrad was the first mayor of Fort Benton and lost a U.S. Senate race by one vote.

*Above:* Home of T.C. Power, merchant prince and U.S. Senator from Montana

## Municipal Government

From late 1862, when the first buildings went up outside the fort, it was twenty-one years before a municipal government was formed. An election was held on April 2, 1883 and the City of Fort Benton came into being. The vote to incorporate was 58 for, 28 against; some of the old ways still remained hidden in the back streets. Running unopposed, William G. Conrad was elected mayor with 86 votes. Fort Benton exceeded the status of a town; the census of 1880 showed a population of over 1600, well above the 1000

for city status. It was the third largest city in Montana Territory behind Butte and Helena. The city had been called Benton, Fort Benton and Benton City at various times. According to the local newspaper almost every state had a Benton, but there was only one Fort Benton in the whole wide world. Fort Benton received its name in an official municipal proclamation, and is still the only place in the whole wide world with

*Top*: *Freight on the Fort Benton levee during the last years of the steamboat trade*

*Below: Spring 1886 with the City of Fort Benton still on the bank from winter, and remains of the ice flow that slightly damaged her*

*Left:* St. Clair Montefalco Hospital, 1886 - 1974

# Public Buildings

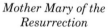

Sister Anna Magnan

Mother Mary of the Resurrection

Sister Mary Wilfred

*Above:* Three founding Sisters of Providence

*Left*: Fort Benton School built in 1884, burned in 1937

## Finally a Bridge Across the River

The first ferry was built in 1875, and Al Smith was the first ferryman. Wagons on the Graham Wagon Road to mines in the southern mountains were frequent customers. In 1878 Castner and Smith built a 75-foot hull that could carry two six-mule teams and wagons at a time. Lynch and Flint entered the competition in 1881 with the Baker Street Ferry, and by 1883 Malcolm Morrow Sr. had a third ferry operating on the levee.

After several years of ferries and fording the river at the lower end of town, in 1887-1888 local merchants financed the first bridge across the Missouri, providing ready access to markets in the Judith Basin and Meagher County. There was still an illusion of reviving steamboat trade so the first span was a turn span that opened to allow boat passage. Only two boats ever passed through, and they were on pleasure excursions. The bridge soon put ferries out of business. Even a toll levied at the bridge did not offset the time factor, the ferrys' irregular schedules and their seasonal operation.

*Top: Steamer OK and the swing span; only the OK and the Josephine ever passed through.*

*Below: The new bridge put the Baker Street Ferry out of business.*

*Bottom: Levee in 1885 when trade was over. Baker Street Ferry's cable tower is visible.*

# Main Street Business

**Top:** *Shop of Gus Senieur, builder of the Courthouse*

**Above:** *Baker and DeLorimer's General Merchandise Store was later Fort Benton's first movie theater.*

**Above:** *Dan Dutro's Studio, Fort Benton photographer of the 1870's-1880's*

**Left:** *New brick First National Bank in 1882; Pres Lewis's mule train is out front ready to head up the Whoop-Up Trail.*

# The River Press
## 1880 to the Present

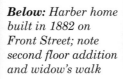

**Above:** Press room with the large steam press ready to put out the latest edition

**Below:** Harber home built in 1882 on Front Street; note second floor addition and widow's walk

**Above:** River Press' first editor, Jeremiah Collins

**Above:** The River Press after it moved from an adobe building on Main Street to the Moffitt Saddlery on Front Street

**Below:** W.K. Harber, editor of the River Press from 1891 to 1922

*Top:* Circuit-riding Bishop T. Tuttle, first Episcopal Bishop of Montana

*Above:* St. Paul's Episcopal Church in 1880, oldest church in Fort Benton and oldest Episcopal Church in Montana

*Above:* Interior of St. Paul's showing 1880's altar and chancel

*Lower left:* First Catholic Church of the Immaculate Conception, built in 1879 and burned in 1906

# First Fort Benton Churches

*Below:* Methodist Church under construction, built by Brother Van Orsdel; in the distance is the Metropolitan Hotel.

## First in Lights and Water

On March 17, 1888 the Geo. F. Woolston Water Works and Electric Light Plant turned on the juice from a steam-powered plant, and over a dozen businesses on Front Street lit up in a blaze of light. It was just six years after Edison developed his first central power station. Fort Benton was the first city in Montana to have municipal lights and water, a month ahead of Helena and many months before Butte.

## End of the Steamboats

When the railroad arrived in 1887, most commercial river traffic ceased. Small locally-constructed boats like the *Baby Rose, City of Fort Benton* and *OK* still made runs along the upper river, carrying supplies and taking on produce. After the turn-of-the-century isolated homesteaders living along the river relied on their service. As homes on the secluded bottoms were gradually abandoned, river traffic eventually disappeared. It was much easier to

*Right:* The building boom came to an end in 1893 with construction of the New Overland Hotel.

*Above:* Interior of the lobby-restaurant of the New Overland Hotel in later years

live "up on top" with ready access to the newly-constructed roads.

In 1921 the last steamboat from downriver docked in Fort Benton. Long after commercial travel vanished the *Mandan*, owned by the U.S. Corps of Engineers, made an annual trip to Fort Benton; its mission was removal of snags from the river. It was a government "pork barrel," with no apparent reason for its service.

The end of an era left behind memories of a glorious past. . . the cry "steamboat 'round the bend!", a deep steam whistle announcing its arrival and the

excited crowd gathering on the levee to greet the first boat of the season.

## The Finale

The Canadian Pacific to the north and Northern Pacific to the south skirted Fort Benton as they pushed toward the Pacific in 1883. The business community realized that railroads would ruin their commercial empires; trains delivered passengers and freight more quickly and cheaper than any riverboat. Fort Benton's merchants lobbied the Northern Pacific while track was being laid west of Bismarck. They wanted the rails to turn north through Judith Gap to Fort Benton then over Marias Pass to the coast. They lost that fight in favor of Butte and her mines. The river trade survived one more season before its commerce began to collapse.

Track was not laid to Fort Benton until 1887 when the Great Northern Railroad brought an-

*Left:* The Baby Rose, built in 1909 at Fort Benton by Charles Crepeau, was crushed by the ice that same winter. Her hull can still be seen against the bank below the Lewis and Clark Memorial.

# The Last Fort Benton Steamboats

*Above:* Steamboat OK, freight and tour boat, was brought to Fort Benton by owner "Cap" Geo. Stevens in 1907. She hauled freight as far downriver as Wilder's Landing and made two excursions upriver. The OK burned on the bank of the Fort Benton levee June 30, 1908, some say for insurance purposes.

*Left:* City of Fort Benton, the smallest steamboat on the upper river, was used as a dredge boat. Built in 1885, she burned at the Judith in 1892.

*Top: Great Northern at the Teton Station coal stop, next stop Fort Benton*

other transcontinental road across Montana. River commerce aided its own demise by hauling supplies for the railroads. Perhaps from spite, Fort Benton would not allow the rails to come into town; the siding was built out on the prairie. The silver spike was driven clear through the heart of Fort Benton's commerce when festivities on the hill celebrated the railroad's reaching the head of navigation on the Missouri River.

The open range cattle and sheep industry was all that kept Fort Benton alive through the turn-of-the-century. The last of the building boom occurred in 1893 when Fort Benton's first hotel, the Overland, was torn down to build a new one. It was rumored that the owner panned dirt from under the old floors, and found enough gold dust to build a three-story hotel rather than two.

Fort Benton slipped quietly into the 20th century. Precious little was left of its boisterous past, and only a lingering memory remained of its historic heritage. The Birthplace of Montana is recognized as a National Historic Landmark for its national importance to Western Expansion during the last half of the 19th century.

*Right: Old Fort Benton in the 1890's. The blockhouse is the last remaining building, about ready to fall in this photo.*

*Chapter 7*

# The Open Range

*Free Grass! Cattle replaced buffalo as they disappeared from the open range. Stockmen built huge ranches with thousands of cattle until the winter of 1886-1887 when disaster struck the Montana range.*

## Cattle Saved a Depressed Economy

As the river trade closed in 1887 and the first train whistled for the siding on the hill above Fort Benton, the surrounding country was filling with cattle. They arrived in the mid-1870's, only a few at first then by the thousands during the mid-1880's. Cattlemen were recuperating from the winter disaster in 1886-87, and Fort Benton was making a last ditch attempt to save itself as a transportation center.

## Bridge Across the River

To shore up their sagging economy, the merchants of Fort Benton formed the Benton Bridge Company. The largest market they wanted to capture was the wool business that had developed in the Judith Basin and in Meagher County. The new company was headed by W.G. Conrad, who built a

*Below: First bridge across the Missouri River in Montana; the span on the left is a swing span to permit boat passage.*

*Left: Cattle grazing on the open range of the Shonkin in the 1880's*

*Right: Charlie Russell on one of his frequent visits to Fort Benton with one of his many friends, Dave Frields*

concrete warehouse to store wool for shipment either by rail or by boat from Fort Benton.

Money for the bridge was raised by public subscription. After six months the company had raised or had subscriptions for $65,000 to complete the structure. In January 1888 contracts were let to the Milwaukee Bridge Works for steel trusses and superstructure, and piers and approaches to Ryan and Henry. Plans called for three truss spans of 175 feet each and a small span of 65 feet. The design included a swinging span of 225 feet and three ice breakers of wood upstream in front of the piers. Construction began in March and the bridge was opened to traffic in mid-December 1888. The privately-owned structure was a toll bridge until it was sold to Chouteau County in 1896 for $9999.99; the unusual price was to beat government red tape!

Fort Benton's bridge is Montana's most significantly historic. It is the first vehicular bridge in Montana to span the Missouri, the first all steel truss bridge in Montana and the oldest steel bridge in the state.

## Illegal Aliens

In 1891 another aspect of business opportunities came to light. Enterprising Bentonites were smuggling Orientals into the United States from Canada. One incident made the newspapers in August, but it is likely that it was only one of many.

The paper reported that Gus Brede was killed by lightning in a wagon coming down into the Teton Valley toward Fort Benton. He was supposedly seated between two Chinese who were unscathed, called "justice in a lightning bolt." Authorities also found nine more Chinese hidden beneath the tarpaulin in the overturned wagon. They had been smuggled out of Fort Macleod and were summarily deported. The location gained its name for eternity, Chinamen Hill.

Brede was quite an enterprising fellow. He found a lucrative two-way trip between the two forts. Brede had previously been arrested and fined $1000 by the Mounties for smuggling whiskey into Canada, and had already lost one outfit to U.S. Customs for smuggling Chinese. Some things never seemed to change in Fort Benton's business!

## The Last of the Buffalo

No one realized in 1879, when the Blackfoot invited Joe Kipp and James Willard Schultz to the range between the Missouri and Yellowstone, that it would be the last bison hunt of Native Americans in the United States. Over four thousand animals were taken that fall. Before the hunt was over, the Indians were forced

back to their reservation by the military. Never again was the robe trade a profitable venture. Kipp described the end: "I was born in the buffalo trade, I expected to die in it. The buffalo are gone, I don't know what to do." With the disappearance of the buffalo in eastern Montana by 1880, cattle took over the open range and the free grass.

## The Beginnings

It is likely that the first cattle in the area were milk cows at the fort brought in by fur traders. Most fur posts had barns and a collection of domestic farm animals. From 1830 to 1860 most bovines were used to produce

*Below: Front Street in the 1890's with the Stockmen's National Bank, Gans and Klein, and Murphy Maclay and Co. in the uptown business district*

*Above: Fort Benton's famous saddlery shop of Jos. Sullivan, who once built 500 western-style saddles for the North West Mounted Police*

*Top right: Johnny Grant, Montana's first cattleman, raised herds in the Deer Lodge Valley.*

*Below: Moving cattle onto the eastern Montana range*

butter, cream and milk. Chouteau and Company's inventory for Fort Benton in the spring of 1851 showed two oxen, seven cows and calves and ten pigs. In the early 1860's Chouteau and Company had a few hundred cattle pastured across the river near the fort. They were probably draft animals to pull the many wagons used in the robe trade at Fort Benton.

Thanks to the Oregon Trail, Fort Hall in Idaho became a trade center for trail-worn cattle and oxen. Traders swapped one healthy animal that had been nursed back to health for two that couldn't

make it any further down the trail. As the size of those herds increased, they were moved north into the Deer Lodge Valley for winter pasture and returned the next spring for sale or trade. The Grant brothers, who were occasional visitors in Fort Benton, pioneered this first cattle business and were the first to bring herds into Montana.

## Trail Drives and Early Markets

At the beginning of the gold rush in 1862, two enterprising young men, Konrad Kohrs and John Bielenberg, saw a ready market for beef in the gold camps exploding with humanity. They went to Oregon and trailed a herd of cattle into the Deer Lodge Valley. By 1865 D.A.G. Floweree had brought a large herd from Missouri. With Nelson Story's drive of 1000 head from Texas in 1866, the cattle business in Montana began to expand. Through the

1860's dairy and beef markets in Montana were strictly local: the large gold camps at Bannack, Virginia City and Helena and the military posts that were established in the early 1870's.

Most of the cattle were trailed in from Oregon to stock the small Montana herds. Small ranches were started by dis-gruntled miners who had found little of the "yellow stuff" but enough to buy a few cows. They went into business by selling butter, cream and beef to their fellow miners. ·

By 1870 the cattle business was starting to grow in northern Montana, and in the Fort Benton area herds increased by leaps and bounds. Texas cattle were bought by local cattlemen and trailed to Montana in large numbers. Robert S. Ford, Tom Dunn, Burd and Sons, D.A.G. Floweree and John Cox began stocking the Sun River Valley in 1872. One must remember that it was still a lawless land. Blackfoot war parties and marauding outlaws made the cattle business very precarious.

Ranchers needed markets close to home; it was much too far

*Left:* *To get his start, Konrad Kohrs sold beef, butter and cream to miners in the gold camps at Bannack and Virginia City.*

*Left:* *Center Market. W.S. Stocking, W.H. Burgess and Ed Kelly also operated early Fort Benton butcher shops that supplied the local market with beef.*

to drive herds to market in the East. The only access to Eastern markets in the early years was by driving the cattle to Fort Benton then shipping them by steamboat down the Missouri River, a better alternative than the long exhausting trek south and east to a railhead. However, neither was a profitable option.

The transcontinental railroad was completed in 1869, but still meant trail drives of over 1000 miles to Ogden or Cheyenne. According to promoters indulging in hypothetical accounting, a cattleman who drove 1000 head of four-year-old steers to market could clear $40,000 on the sale of his herd. Note that no mention was made of the risky trail through Indian Country!

It was not until the railroads came to Montana that small herds multiplied on the eastern plains. Montana cattlemen finally had an accessible profitable market.

*Above:* Robert S. Ford, leader of the Sun River Rangers

*Top:* Most early bovines at Fort Benton were draft animals for the many wagons.

*Upper right:* Early northern Montana cowboys; standing upper right is C.J. Streit

*Below:* Officers' Row at Fort Shaw, an early market for cattlemen

## Sun River Rangers

In 1874 ranchers on the Sun River banded together to protect their open range herds from rustlers. The Sun River Rangers were the first livestock association in Montana. Cattle rustling had only two penalties, a bullet or a rope, no questions asked. The organization was the model for others that came into existence as new ranges opened across Montana and problems developed.

## Fort Benton Cattle

The first ranch in the Fort Benton area was established in 1867-1868 by Winfield S. Stocking on the Teton about three miles from town. With the ever-present

110

danger of Indian raids, the ranch had a stockade of sorts and an escape tunnel to the river bank. Stocking created his own market by furnishing beef to his own meat market in Fort Benton.

By 1871-1872 James Arnoux, Roland Buckland and John Harris had established cattle ranches along Highwood Creek in the foothills of the Highwood Mountains. During the early 1870's some of Fort Benton's eventually prominent cattlemen were starting their ranches in the mountain valleys around gold camps and military forts. John Lepley, Malcolm Morrow and his three sons Malcolm Jr., William T. and David had small places on Little Prickly Pear Creek. They had panned gold from Silver Creek and turned it into cattle. In 1873 their first brand was registered in Lewis and Clark County. Helena and Fort Shaw probably provided markets for their animals before they left the valleys.

*Above: Established in 1865, the Stocking Ranch on the Teton was Chouteau County's first ranch. Note its fort-like appearance.*

## New Ranges Open Up

During the mid-1870's cattlemen began to move from mountain valleys surrounding the mining camps onto the prairies. The Sun, Marias, Teton and Shonkin ranges near Fort Benton opened up when the U.S. government reclaimed Indian lands with new treaties. Cattle began to share the eastern prairies with bison. Cattlemen soon realized that bison ate the grass that their cattle grazed on. Wandering Indian tribes were also a menace to the cattle industry. Cattlemen promoted the quick removal of both from the plains.

*Left: Winfield Scott Stocking came to Fort Benton as a cattleman and meat market operator.*

## The Shonkin

In 1877 John Lepley moved his herd from Rocky Gap near Cascade onto the Shonkin Range. He had been in partnership with C.H. Austin who took his share of the herd into the Chestnut Valley. During the next two years A.W. Kingsbury, M.E. Milner and his partner John Boardman moved into the Shonkin.

Three of the stockmen started trailing in cattle and shorthorn bulls from Oregon to improve their herds. In those first years the three bachelors kept their bulls in a pasture near one of the ranches, and lived together for mutual protection . . . for the animals and for themselves.

Malcolm Morrow Sr. left his claims on Little Prickly Pear Creek in 1878 and headed to the Shonkin Range with his family and three adult sons. They settled along Shonkin Creek and the Missouri River. The Morrows had been early neighbors of John Lepley on the Little Prickly Pear, and renewed their friendship on the Shonkin range.

There were still buffalo on those early ranges even though hide hunters were rapidly depleting their numbers. Buffalo meant wandering parties of Blackfoot off the reservation, hunting and creating problems for lone cowboys on the range.

## Cattle Become Big Business

Two railroads, the Canadian Pacific to the north in Calgary and the Northern Pacific across southern Montana, opened the vast cattle ranges to national markets by 1883. Herds expanded across most of eastern Montana. Thousands of animals were driven to the railheads, loaded into stock cars and taken to markets in Chicago and Omaha.

The Shonkin Stock Association was formed in 1881. Its range included land south of the Missouri, west of the Judith Basin and north of the Highwood Mountains. The Marias Roundup formed northwest of Fort Benton at a later date. Officers of the various associations included prominent cattlemen. Konrad Kohrs, Robert Ford, Granville Stuart, Henry Sieben and Robert Colburn hailed from nearby ranges. The Shonkin Asso-

# SHONKIN STOCK ASSOCIATION
# ROUNDUP

**Shonkin Stock Association at the Spring Coulee Corrals, 1886**
*Left to right: T.A. Cummings, Tingley, Tom Healey, John Green, Sam Kohlberg, John Lepley, John Rice, Martin Connolly, Tim Collins, Dick Mee, R.S. Tingley, Malcolm Morrow Sr., Ike Clark, Joe Tatsie, Joe Tromley. On fence: Malcolm Morrow Jr., an unknown cowboy, George Frields, Jake Becker, Wm. T. Morrow*

**Above:** *Chow time at the cook tent during spring roundup*

**Above right:** *John Lepley and Malcolm Morrow tallying calves in the Spring Coulee Corrals*

**Right:** *Horse remuda with cowboys getting a new mount for the day*

113

*Top: Open range cattle during the 1880's of the Shonkin and Marias Associations in northern Montana*

*Below right: John Lepley on his favorite black horse, dressed as most cattlemen in suit and tie even on the range*

*Below: Malcolm Morrow Sr. started in the gold camps then moved to the Shonkin Range in the 1870's.*

ciation was masterminded by M. E. Milner, Secretary. Other officers included Jack Harris, John Lepley, A.W. Kingsbury and Malcolm Morrow.

William and Charles Conrad's Circle outfit was the largest on the Marias range. Jack Harris, Ed Kelly, Fred LaBarre and Captain Nels Veilleaux also ran stock in the Teton and Marias valleys.

Activities of the associa-

tions centered in and around Fort Benton; the Grand Union Hotel was their unofficial headquarters. In 1889 Association members established the Stockmen's National Bank for their financial interests. The bank thrived until the homestead era.

Associations staged a spring and a fall roundup. The number of cowboys from each ranch was based upon the number of cattle bearing their particular brand. In the spring cattle were herded to various sites on the range where new calves were branded with the brand of their mothers. Cows and calves from other ranches were branded and returned to their home range by the "Reps," cowboys sent by other associations to return their wandering stock. During fall roundup, market cattle were cut from the herd and strays were branded.

## Texas Cattle

Abundant free Montana grass was exceptionally nutritious as it cured in the late summer sun. It provided an excellent source of winter food for cattle, if winter weather did not prevent cattle from reaching it.

The range was so good, and there was so much open prairie available that Texas outfits began to invade eastern Montana with

trail herds in the 1880's. When the Judith Basin opened, eastern Montana south of the Missouri experienced a tremendous influx of cattle from Texas and the Southwest. The new outfits took over the Miles City Ranges and moved strongly into the Judith Basin with their herds, but were stymied from any further penetration by the Shonkin Stock Association.

For mutual protection Association stockmen had homesteaded all the water sites and roundup sites on their range, and prohibited use by non-members . . . and their membership was closed. The Association threatened interlopers with fenced ranges and thirsty Texas herds if they moved onto their range. The threat (or bluff) was effective. There were no Texas cattle on the Shonkin range unless they carried the brand of an Association member.

*Above:* David G. Browne: bullwhacker, merchant, ferry operator, and President of the Stockmen's National Bank

*Top left:* Stockmen's National Bank, founded in 1889 by local cattlemen, later became the Chouteau County Bank.

*Inset:* Home of banker David G. Browne; he founded Old Fort Park that surrounded the original fort.

*Left:* John Harris, first president of the Shonkin Association and boss of the Circle Outfit on the Marias-Teton Range

*Right:* Granville Stuart, cattleman in the Judith Basin and leader of the Vigilantes in the Missouri Breaks

It appears that Milton Milner was a shrewd "wheeler dealer." Through his efforts, the Association discouraged additional cattle on their range by limiting membership. Cattlemen gained entry only by buying out an Association member. Line fences put up by the Association discouraged nesters' cattle from drifting out of the mountains onto the Shonkin range. Fences remained even into the early homestead era, preventing "honyoker" cattle on ranges the various associations considered to be their holdings.

## Vigilantes in the Breaks

*Below:* Shorthorns brought from Oregon to improve the breed on the Shonkin and Marias ranges

Associations handled their own range problems such as rustlers and wolves. Bounties were paid on wolves; dogs were sometimes purchased to hunt them. In 1884 rustlers were taking quite a toll on herds in the Shonkin and the Judith Basin. Directed by officers of both associations and led by Granville Stuart, vigilante

groups were organized. They cleaned out the trouble with fire and lead, . . . and thirteen knotted ropes.

According to their minutes, a request had been made by the Judith Basin Association for assistance from the Shonkin Stock Association. The minutes indicated that full cooperation would be extended. There is no written record of what action was to be taken nor any mention in later minutes of the problem. However, in the *River Press* a few weeks later it was reported that a "group of cowboys" hanged rustlers along the river.

The Missouri Breaks formed the northern boundary of their ranges. Beyond the river were Indian reservations which provided a haven for wolfers, rustlers and desperadoes. The region was an early hangout for Butch Cassidy and the Sundance Kid (Kid Curry). It was also home to the infamous Pike Landusky, who was shot by Kid Curry in 1894.

## Disaster Strikes

The summer of 1886 had been extremely dry. The range was not only depleted by the weather but also by many cattle that had been brought in during the past year. Cattlemen were concerned that the range would not carry them through the winter, and were hoping for minimal losses when disaster struck.

Winter arrived early and stayed late in 1886-1887. In the early weeks there were particularly heavy snows with little wind. Grazing animals had to paw and nuzzle down through deep snow to feed. A chinook in January changed the snow to ice, as it does quite often on the high plains. All natives know Montana weather is unpredictable at best!

At the end of January a terrible blizzard blew in from the north, bringing temperatures averaging well below -20 degrees that even reached -63 degrees in some places. A crust of ice formed on the snow that hooves and noses could not penetrate. Starving animals froze in their tracks. As icy winds swirled across the Montana plains, animals died by the thousands. There was no relief for weeks. When the weather finally broke and warm chinook winds blew in, more than half of the cattle were dead and so was the open range cattle industry.

With major changes in their operations, some cattlemen survived until the homesteaders arrived. The cattle that made it were depicted in Charlie Russell's "Waiting for a Chinook." The gaunt-ribbed "barely alives" wandered through spring, and by roundup looked like cattle again. The spring calf count on the Marias and Shonkin ranges was down over 50% from the previous season. Amazingly, the following year it rebounded back to nearly normal numbers.

Local stockmen put up hay and reduced their herds to a manageable level for winter care. Recovery came soon. The next winter was mild, spring rainfall was ample, and a good calf crop returned prosperity. Since the supply of beef was sharply reduced, prices rose and cattlemen who survived were back on their feet in a short time.

*Top: "Waiting for a Chinook" or "The Last of the Five Thousand." The winter of 1886-1887 brought an end to the open range. Charlie Russell's graphic portrayal of those that managed to survive tells the story.*

*Bottom: Putting up hay for winter feed became a way of life for stockmen after the winter of 1886-1887.*

*Above: Marias Association at a water stop. L to R: Bob Sterling, Gilbert Embleton, Frank Sterling, Chas. Brinkman, unknown cowboy, Louis Lundy, Jim Guardipee and Frank Kelly*

# Marias - Teton Range

The Marias Range was north to the Canadian border and west of Fort Benton on both sides of the river. With the Circle Outfit,

*Top right: Ed Kelly: operator of 28-Mile Stage Station, merchant in Fort Benton and cattleman on the Teton Range*

*Above: Branding on the Teton during spring roundup*

*Below: Marias Roundup at Bull Head Coulee in the spring of 1880*

Ed Kelly, Fred LaBarre, the Tingley brothers and D.A.G. Floweree were running cattle and horses on the Marias. They held a common roundup and shared range problems. Probably the first large herd in the area belonged to Floweree; he brought his herds from other ranges to this northern range. Floweree was not only a stockman, but also had large interests in freighting on the Montana frontier.

In 1879 Jessie Taylor brought 2500 head to the Teton. Ryan and Dunphy came with another 1100, and John Drew brought in a large herd of pure bred cattle. John and Howell Harris, Matt Carroll and Floweree were also adding to their stock.

After he was President of the Shonkin Stock Association in 1881, John Harris and his brother Howell joined the cattle business owned by the Conrad Brothers and C.W. Price. The Montana and St. Louis Cattle Company resulted, and the company's cattle were moved to the Marias Range.

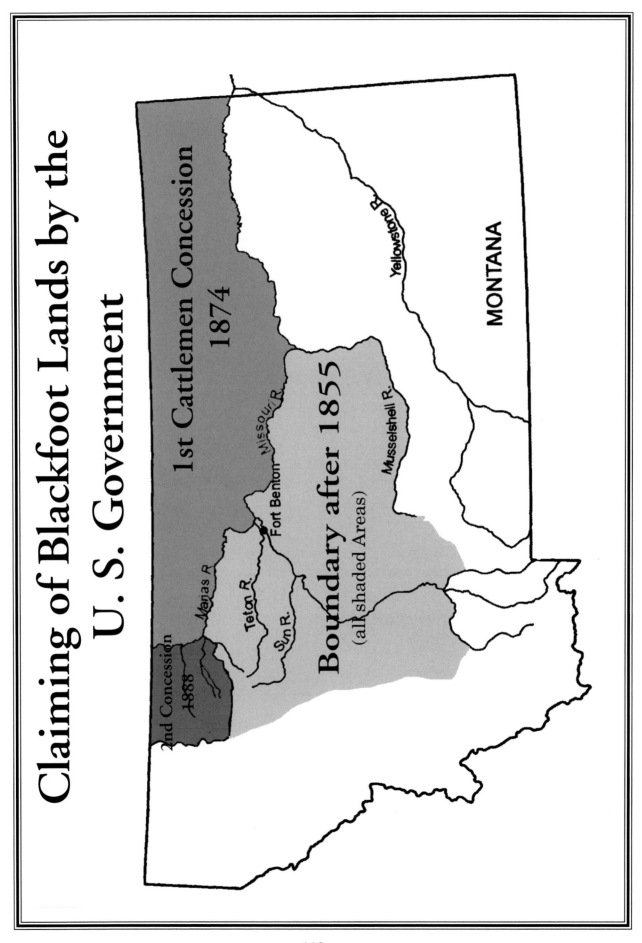

Claiming of Blackfoot Lands by the U. S. Government

1st Cattlemen Concession 1874

2nd Concession 1888

Boundary after 1855
(all shaded Areas)

Marias R.

Teton R.

Sun R.

Missouri R.

Fort Benton

Musselshell R.

Yellowstone R.

MONTANA

*Right:* *T.C. Power & Bro.'s harness display for wagons and their teams of horses and mules*

## The Circle Outfit

The largest cattle outfit in the area was the Benton and St. Louis Cattle Company, later called the Conrad Circle Cattle Company. It was organized in 1882 on land "squatted on" by C.W. Price, the Conrad brothers' brother-in-law. Price's herd was consolidated with cattle from the Harris Cattle

*Right:* *C.W. Price: cattleman on the Marias Range, brother-in-law of W.G. and C.E. Conrad and a partner in the Circle Outfit*

Company of Highwood to form the new company's herd. John Harris was manager of operations south of the Canadian border; his brother Howell managed the Canadian herd. Stockholders in the company included W.G. Conrad, C.E. Conrad, C.W. Price, Joseph A. Baker and the Harris brothers.

Ranch headquarters was on the Maria's River, where Montana Highway 200 crosses the river north of Fort Benton today. Their Canadian headquarters was near High River in Alberta. The company ran from fifteen to twenty-five thousand head of cattle south of the border, and branded between two to five thousand calves each year. Their northern herd was comparable in size.

The Circle Outfit's Marias Range extended from the Missouri north to the International Boundary, east to Fort Belknap and west as far as the Sun River. Their Canadian range extended from the Rocky Mountains in the west, to the Cypress Hills in the east and

from the border north into the High River country.

The company's markets included Indian contracts on both sides of the border, Canadian government contracts with the Mounted Police and contracts with U.S. Military. When the Canadian Pacific railhead reached Lethbridge in 1883, the Chicago market was opened. Their cattle drives were to Montana stockyards when the Great Northern reached Montana in 1887.

The Circle Outfit's cattle bore the circle brand on the left ribs both north and south of the border. Since the two ranges joined across the boundary line, it seems the herds mysteriously drifted back and forth across the border at tax time. The size of the U.S. herd decreased when that count was taken and likewise when the count was made north of the border. After a few years the Canadian government declared that Canadian cattle could not have the same brand as their American counterparts. It was amazing how both herds increased in size the following year.

*Above: Building the railroad in 1887, up the Government Grade out of the Teton River to the Fort Benton Station on top of the hill*

## When the Works All Done in the Fall

A cowboy story is a final tribute to the open range days in Fort Benton. A young cowboy, Edwin Dale, wrote to his parents in May 1899 about his plans to come home the next year. He told them he would be late because of the roundup, but he planned to be home for Christmas and New Year's. In his letter, written while waiting to get started on the roundup, he said there were six outfits in Fort Benton, all ready to begin the roundup in a few days. "There was quite a time in Benton last night. There was about 75 cowboys in there, they were having a hot time I tell you."

The next year a two-line item appeared in the *River Press*. It noted that a cowboy Edwin Dale was shot and killed by William Howell on September 13 over a card table in the McCauley and Colgate Saloon. A blunt telegram was sent by Sheriff C.W. Buck to Dale's father: "Edward Dale died four a.m. Wire instructions." A few days after the murder a coroner's

*Right: Thomas H. Martin, cowpuncher and bullwhacker from Fort Benton and the Shonkin Range*

jury acquitted Howell stating it was self-defense. The lawless ways were not quite dead in Fort Benton.

On October 3, the Executive Committee of the Shonkin Stock Association (M.E. Milner, Charles Lepley, Malcolm Morrow and T.A. Cummings) published a letter that stated Dale's death was blatant murder of an innocent cowboy who worked for the Association. The authorities reconsidered their earlier action, and on November 28 Wm. Howell was charged with second degree murder; later that year he was convicted and sentenced to life imprisonment. Score one for the good guys, maybe a first in Fort Benton's history.

## Mutton and Wool

Unlike Wyoming, sheep peacefully entered the Montana ranges in the 1880's. Since cattlemen also became sheepmen, they coexisted without incident, and found that both animals were compatible on the same range. By the mid 1890's Fort Benton was the biggest shipping point for sheep and wool in Montana. The Montana Woolgrowers were organized in 1883. Benton merchants built a large concrete wool warehouse on the banks of the Missouri in 1888. Both prospered until the region was opened to the Homestead Acts in 1908.

Some credit Father Ravalli with bringing sheep into the Bitterroot in 1847, but the first herd actually recorded was in 1865 when George W. Forbes brought 3500 head into the Virginia City area. When they were shorn,

**Below**: *Blacksmith shop on an old cattle ranch. Note the sharpening tools on the roof.*

*Above: Three men doing the spring shearing. The fleece was loaded into enormous wool sacks and sent to market.*

*Top right: A.E. McLeish, prominent Fort Benton woolgrower*

*Below: Woolies by the thousands with their herder on the northern Montana range*

area. When they were shorn, 21,000 pounds of wool were sent downriver from Fort Benton. Because of its bulk and weight, the only economical way to send wool to market was downriver by steamboat. An early connection was established with area woolgrowers and the concentration of buyers in Fort Benton.

Wool shipped by steamboat rose to 830,000 pounds in 1878. By 1882, with most of the Judith Basin and Meagher County also bringing their wool for shipment, the total reached 1,122,756 pounds.

The area's most prominent sheepman was Henry MacDonald. He was born in Scotland, served in the Civil War, then came West. MacDonald had some exciting years before settling down to raise sheep like many of his native Scots. He was a partner of the Smith Brothers in Meagher County when he hired two young herders in 1882. One was Louis Osnes, who later bought the ranch from his mentor. The other herder was Louis Riel, who lost his flock and in 1885 his life during the Metis Rebellion in Canada. In 1878

*Right: Shearing pens with hand shearers at work on the Shonkin Range*

124

# Homes of Fort Benton's Stockmen

*Above:* John H. Green home under construction in 1910. Green was a cattleman on the Shonkin Range and a banker in Fort Benton.

*Above:* John Harris, who ran the Circle Outfit on the Marias-Teton Range, built his home in 1884.

*Left:* A.E. McLeish home was built in 1910 on the site of the first I.G. Baker Store on Front Street

*Above:* Claus H. Evers home near the river; Evers ran sheep on the Shonkin.

*Left:* John Lepley's home built in 1880 on the Big Sag Ranch

MacDonald came to Chouteau County with 2000 head of Merino sheep and settled on Cottonwood Creek near Round and Square Buttes. His story is well documented by his daughter in *Wandersong*, a must-read book of the area.

MacDonald's neighbor, George D. Patterson, brought in 4000 head purchased from Governor Potts in 1878. Patterson got his start in Judith Gap with the Bower brothers, remembered from the book *Chip of the Flying U.*

Paris Gibson also went into business in Fort Benton; he came to Montana to start over after the Panic of 1873. Gibson ran sheep along Highwood Creek on shares with Henry MacDonald and got back on his feet. Gibson encouraged his friend James J. Hill to purchase a town site near the Great Falls of the Missouri in 1884, and became the first mayor of Great Falls. When T. C. Power held out for more money for a right-of-way through Fort Benton, the railroad tracks bypassed the town by going up on the hill. According to legend, Gibson said, "I'll see grass growing in the streets of Fort Benton," and he almost did.

One of Fort Benton's largest sheepmen was A. E. McLeish. He had woolies on several ranges, especially in the Bear's Paw Mountains. McLeish's wife Dorothy was

*Left:* Wool wagons headed to Fort Benton, the state's largest wool shipper

prominent in the Fort Benton Women's Club, and was a prime mover in building the Carnegie Library in the 1920's.

## Wool Revived Business Interests

Fort Benton's wool business continued to grow. The I.G. Baker Company was the primary dealer; their warehouse stored wool for shipment by boat, later by rail. This landmark stood until 1936 when the WPA tore it down in favor of a swimming pool. In 1897

there were half a million sheep in Chouteau County. The peak of 800,000 was reached in 1903. When homesteaders poured into the country after 1908, the range declined. The last years of prosperity were during World War I.

From the beginning sheep were part of Fort Benton business; the river was the only reasonable means of transport for the bulky sacks of wool. In 1883 the Montana Woolgrowers Association was formed, where else but in the Grand Union Hotel in Fort Benton. Paris Gibson was elected President and L.W. Peck, Secretary. The Association believed Fort Benton was the best wool market in the Territory. The next July the second convention was held, again at the hotel, and George D. Patterson was elected President. The love affair between the Woolgrowers and Fort Benton continued through the 1890's.

## Turn-of-the-Century

As the twentieth century approached, Fort Benton had quieted to a slow walk. Law and order had finally arrived, society had changed from merchants to

*Above:* Jos. Sullivan's saddle shop was open until his death in 1940.

*Left:* Chouteau County Commissioners 1888-1891 were all cattlemen. Seated left: Wm. R. Ralston. Standing: David G. Brown. Seated right: John Harris

127

*Top: 1894 on Front Street, the inaugural Johnston Stage Line's (notice flag on coach) trip to Lewistown with Oscar Johnston up*

stockmen, and new businesses had come to town with the cattle and sheep. Fort Benton remained as progressive as it had always been. The County Commissioners were all stockmen. Jos. Sullivan gradually converted his business to accommodate the beginning farming interests. The town had a telephone exchange and the old frame Choteau House had a new brick front, a large addition and a

new bar.

After their departure in 1881, the U.S. Army continued to return for summer bivouac next to the old fort. Parades, their tent city and an increase in the saloon business were always welcomed by the citizenry.

The Johnston Stage Line was established in 1894 and ran coaches from Fort Benton via the newly-opened bridge to Lone Tree,

*Above and Right: The Army returned for a summer stay in Fort Benton, camping on the flats near Signal Point and periodically parading on the streets.*

*Above: Army ambulance parked in front of a Fort Benton store to pick up supplies during their summer bivouac*

Geyser, Winchell Springs and on to Lewistown. The line operated until 1904 when the "Jawbone Line" brought rails into Lewistown, ending the long distance mail route by stage.

In the 1890's brass bands were popular in Western frontier towns and Fort Benton was no exception. Tom Todd, who seemed to be in the middle of every civic project that occurred in Fort Benton (the volunteer fire department and building the new bridge to mention a few), organized the Fort Benton Brass Band and was its Drum Major. At the turn-of-the-century Fort Benton had the Treasure State Band and in 1903 a gazebo was built in Old Fort Park for concerts. The abandoned I.G. Baker store was converted into an Opera House. It appears that Fort Benton never suffered from lack of the arts.

*Above: Fort Benton's first telephone exchange had two operators.*

*Above: New Choteau House in 1900 with its brick front and new addition with the bar*

*Left: Fort Benton's Brass Band: drum major, Tom Todd; leader, Frank Clark; members: Clause Peters, John Hunsberger, Fred Glinke, William Wolffe, Reuben Archer, Tom Hunsberger, John F. Murphy and John Senieur*

*Right:* Old Fort Benton just after the turn-of-the-century when the Daughters of the American Revolution began restoration

*Insert:* The way it looked in the late 1890's before restoration

become 160- and 320-acre farms belonging to the horde of homesteaders who settled the region from 1908 to 1920. It was the end of the big cattle herds and sheep bands. They were either sold off or moved north of the Missouri. The open range gave way to a milk cow or two with a bum lamb in a homesteader's pasture.

*Above:* The blacksmith was nearly done; cars, trucks and garages were about to take over. Emil Breault was a local smithy near the turn-of-the-century.

*Right:* Northern Montana Cattlemen's Association meeting on Main Street was the "last hurrah" before the open range was gone.

130

*Chapter 8*

# People by the Thousands

*They came by the thousands, mostly on the railroads that promoted a better life with free land, dry-land farming and the promise of Utopia. The land was harsh and quickly took its toll; only the hardy survived the long cold winters and the hot summer droughts.*

## Saving the Last Remnant

Next to the Museum of the Upper Missouri in Fort Benton is Montana's oldest standing building. The original bastion of the fur and military post of Fort Benton was built in 1846; there has been no reconstruction of its walls or timbered roof. The blockhouse was saved in 1906 by the Daughters of the American Revolution, who funded stabilization of the walls and base, a new roof and a stucco cover on wire over the exterior. What tremendous insight they had into saving our history! Without their timely intervention, the blockhouse would have been lost forever, and the last original remains of the fur trade would have disappeared from the Montana scene.

## The Rush into the New Century

At the beginning of the new century Fort Benton stepped back and took a look at itself, marveled at its past, and jumped into the next hundred years. A decade of commercial growth occurred. A new high school was built in 1901 before the dramatic changes of the agricultural revolution.

John J. Healy rushed off to the Klondike just before the end of the century to the last of the big gold strikes. His Irish compatriot, Jere Sullivan, rebuilt the Choteau House in 1903 and added a third story a few years later during the homestead boom.

**Top:** *Old fort at the turn-of-the-century*

**Below:** *Rebuilt brick Choteau House.* **Inset:** *Owner Jere Sullivan*

131

The railroad finally came closer to town, after being spurned in 1887 when tracks were not permitted through town. A tunnel was cut through the Crocondunez, and the most expensive piece of track on the entire line was laid along the shale cliffs of the Missouri to a new depot at the edge of Fort Benton. All in all, it took two thousand workers and triggered a short burst of prosperity for the town.

In the northeast corner of the county on July 3, 1901 Kid Curry, Harry Longabaugh and Ben Kirkpatrick held up the Great Northern. During one of Montana's few train robberies, they tried to relieve Mr. Hill of some of his fortune. Bidding Montana farewell, Curry passed through Fort Benton on his way south and left a memento of the robbery with his friend and depot agent Jim Savage.

In February 1901 the "and Bro." of T.C. Power and Bro. ended. John W. Power died in Fort Benton after running the local operation since the 1870's.

The telephone came to Fort Benton in 1902; the town already had public electricity, water and sewer. At the request of the descendants of Pierre and Charles Chouteau, who had lived with the misspelling for forty years, the legislature officially changed the spelling of Choteau County by adding the second "u" in 1903.

In 1906 Charles N. Pray of Fort Benton was elected to the U.S. House of Representatives; he was re-elected for two more terms. Pray was responsible for changes in the Enlarged Homestead Act that made free land more accessible. He also sponsored the act that established Glacier National Park.

Built in 1879, the first frame Church of the Immaculate Conception burned in 1906. It was replaced by a stone church of Swiss Chalet architecture.

The last of the commercial steamboats, the *OK*, came to the levee in 1907 with only 59 tons. It was a mere remnant of the Coulson, Baker and Block P packets from the early era that had established Fort Benton as the "World's Innermost Port."

## From Grass to Grain

At the start of the new century, Fort Benton enjoyed its last boom . . . in people. Farmers invaded the open range and took up homesteads on the short grass prairie. Barbed wire, fences, 160- and 320-acre farms replaced thousands of acres of open range. The land was claimed by young people who "proved up" on their new homes in the West.

In 1908 two floods occurred. In June the streets were filled with water. The flood that lasted for several years filled the streets with homesteaders who populated the rich lands and changed the entire economy of Fort Benton to agriculture. At first row crops of potatoes and corn were planted, then small grains of barley and wheat. The

first flood was dramatic, lasting only a few days and soon forgotten; the second changed the land and the economy forever.

## Montana's Venice

In June 1908, after days and days of rain and snow melt in the mountains, the Missouri River became a torrent. Pressure at the Black Eagle Falls dam reached such proportions that it took out the headgates and powerhouse of the smelting and refining company, and a tide of water rushed toward Fort Benton. The river below the falls widens out so water spread across the bottoms. There was

*Above: New Swiss Chalet style Church of the Immaculate Conception was completed in 1908 before the flood. **Inset**: Ornate altar of the new church*

*Below: The OK, tied up at the Grand Union, only survived one season of sight-seeing on the river. It accidentally burned on the levee the next spring; the insurance payment was great for a bankrupt boat.*

general rising in the actual channel, but by the time the crest reached Fort Benton, the swell overflowed the banks near the present fairgrounds. The river followed its old channel down Franklin Street rather than coming over the levee along Front Street. By early evening of June 5, water flowed through many streets and houses. Water was 6 feet deep around the courthouse; just two blocks away on the levee, the water was only lapping at the doorstep of the Grand Union Hotel. The next morning Front and Main Streets looked like canals in Venice.

Residents retreated to higher ground, dragging their valuable possessions in any conveyance they could find. Through early darkness created by overcast rainy skies, the Michael bell rang out, directing all to safety on the hill behind his Church of the Immaculate Conception. Since his arrival in 1879, Michael the bell had called to the faithful on Sunday and voiced his approval to all

*Below: Height of the June flood in 1908 viewed from the bluffs back of town*

important celebrations and events in Fort Benton.

After two days the water started to recede, and the big clean up began. No one had been lost to the flood waters, but the town's wooden sidewalks had disappeared downriver.

The greatest loss was the old swing span of the 1888 bridge, added in the twilight years of the steamboat age. It was only opened for two boats, the *OK* and the *Josephine*, both on pleasure tours upriver. A working boat never passed through the swing span. Floodwaters undermined the round center pier of the span; the river flow caught its decking and twisted it around the pier like match sticks. The entire superstructure fell into the river. During low water in late summer, remains of the span are still visible between the bank and the first pier.

Shortly after the flood, ferries returned to the Fort Benton levee and operated until a new wooden span was completed eight months after the disaster. A precarious swinging foot bridge closed the gap between the shore and the second span for a short time. In 1927 the temporary wooden span was replaced by a new steel truss to hold heavier vehicular traffic. The old bridge was closed in 1963 and replaced with the Chouteau County Bridge at 13th Street. The new bridge was built with county and federal funds only. The old bridge was reopened to foot traffic in 1982 and today is one of Fort Benton's landmarks.

# Fort Benton Flood 1908

**Above:** *Michael, Fort Benton's famous bell for all occasions*

**Three below:** *Too deep for humans and almost for horses, so find a boat!*

**Above:** *Front Street looking upriver from the fire house*

**Below:** *Front Street from across the river*

**Bottom:** *Front Street downriver from the steps of the Grand Union Hotel*

*Right: When the bridge washed out, the ferries returned. This one is just below the old water plant, heading for its landing at Woodcock's brick mansion across the river.*

Flanagan's Drugstore, the last adobe business building on Front Street, lost its walls to the river and collapsed in the middle. The ruins of old Fort Benton looked like an island in a stormy sea. They stood high and dry above the circling flood waters, the lasting symbol of the city.

## Homestead Acts

The open range disappeared with the arrival of homesteaders seeking free land, and Chouteau County's economy changed from grass to grain. A great land boom erupted in the state in 1908, and the area around Fort Benton was no exception. Under the various homestead acts more people took up more land in Montana than in any other state in the Union. Between 1908 and 1922 there were 114,620 claims filed on 25 million acres. Reclamation and irrigation projects were planned, but the vast acreage of free land, a grand promotional plan by government and railroads, and improved

*Below: Two homes built after the turn-of-the century: Robert F. Brown's, a banker; and George Lewis's, owner of the Livery*

*Left: Swing span at the height of the flood, before the pier dipped and the river grabbed the bridge deck and broke it apart*

# Bridge Washout 1908

*Above: Shortly after the swing span went to the bottom*

*Above and Left: Two views of the walking suspension bridge put in temporarily until the wooden span was built; the wreckage of the swing span and pier are in the river.*

*Above: New wooden span was built in record time of 9 months; it was replaced by Chouteau County with a new steel span in 1927.*

*Right: An appropriate notice above the temporary foot bridge*

137

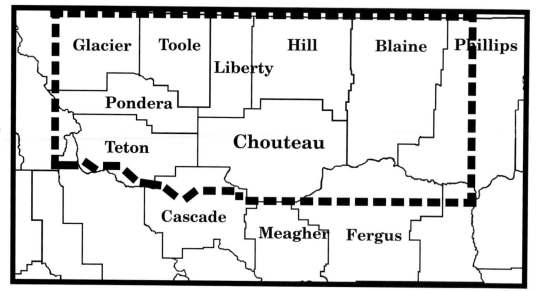

*Right: Dotted line marks the size of Chouteau County in 1884, and the counties that later came completely from or partially from the original county*

farming techniques encouraged dry-land farming.

In 1909 Congress passed the Enlarged Homestead act offering 320 acres, then supplemented the act with a shorter waiting period of three years rather than five. With those changes, land seekers could claim more land and both husband and wife could file thus doubling their holdings. From 1908 until the end of World War I, Chouteau County's population grew from a few hundred people to several thousand. The state's population in 1900 was 243,329; by 1920 after the boom,

Montana had 548,889 people, 57,677 farms and ranches and agriculture was the number one industry replacing mining.

## County-Splitting

The big news just prior to World War I was county-splitting and railroads. Little towns sprang up everywhere as the flood of homesteaders was fueled by railroad and government promotion. Each fledgling town quickly developed a newspaper to sound the praises of its potential as "the

*Right: Front Street about 1900 just before the homestead boom hit the river town: Sullivan Saddlery, the two-story brick Lockwood Drug Store and Sharp Bros.' Department Store*

138

*Left:* Chouteau County Fairgrounds was started during county-splitting.

fastest growing community in the West." Everyone wanted their own county and county seat, and county-splitting became big business. The number of Montana counties grew from 28 in 1910 to 56 in 1925.

Chouteau County, one of Montana's original nine, was split so many times that its area became all or part of eleven new counties. In February 1912 Blaine and Hill Counties split off. Judge Tattan appointed three new county commissioners since the old ones then lived outside Chouteau County.

The next year the county commissioners were directed by

the voters to establish Chouteau County High School and a school in Big Sandy. The Chouteau County Fair started in 1913; the fairgrounds were built next to Roosevelt Island at the upper end of town. 1913 also saw a new railroad in the southern part of the county. The Milwaukee Road was constructed through the Big Sag and established a new town site at Geraldine, named for investor William Rockefeller's daughter. The route connected Great Falls with Lewistown and their transcontinental route coming West.

*Left:* Front Street's River Park with band gazebo for weekly concerts; notice the cast iron light fixtures.

*Above: Fort Benton's first football team; members did not necessarily need to be in school!*

*Below: Horses, wagons, stables and blacksmith shops commanded the streets of Fort Benton at the beginning of the Homestead period.*

# Good Times

At first the weather cooperated. Farmers got forty or more acres of corn, potatoes and grain under cultivation and put up their homestead shacks. Row crops did well since it rained just like it had in the mid-West and the new farmers felt that they had indeed found Utopia. Over 75 per cent of the new arrivals came from mid-Western states, young rural people seeking their fortune and a new life.

They continued to farm much as they had before, and everything went fine until 1914 when the world market for wheat skyrocketed with the outbreak of World War I. For the first time there was money to be made raising grain. Elevators sprang up in every community and steam traction engines appeared. More and more sod was broken to capture the new golden bonanza. By 1916, with the price per bushel at $1.50, farmers had changed to raising grain. During harvest that year the wait at the elevator to unload a grain wagon sometimes lasted for days.

Another Fort Benton first was the first county library in the state. The effort was spearheaded in 1915 by Mrs. A.E. McLeish and the Fort Benton Women's Club, and the library opened in 1916. A Carnegie Foundation grant funded the present structure, completed in

# They Came by Train 1908-1914

**Left:** *Fort Benton Station. Most came with all their worldly goods for a brand new start on the Northern Plains.*

**Above:** *Some came with nothing but a suitcase, the clothes on their back and little in their pocket.*

**Below:** *Livestock tied to the platform were glad to get on solid ground after their long ride from the Midwest.*

**Above:** *With every train arrival, frenzied activity at the depot included masses of horses, cows and people looking for a "320," a bonanza in land instead of gold.*

**Left:** *A whole box car bound for Montana rented for fifty dollars, one-way of course. Notice the two men dressed in suits, ready to take advantage of the "honyockers" as soon as they arrived.*

St. John's the two-story Benton State Bank was built in 1910, the first new commercial establishment in many a year. The Pacific Hotel was remodeled and renamed the Culbertson House. Old time firms took on new wares. Joe Sullivan added farm machinery to his harness, saddle and wagon business, and constructed a new concrete building in 1910. Of course T.C. Power and Bro., who never missed a bet, put in an implement dealership and built a new lumber yard. Their new firm competed with the Missouri River Lumber Co., started in 1910 at the other end of town. Packaged one-room shacks, necessary to legitimize a claim, were a popular purchase. The Missouri River Lumber Co. built its new yard on land that was formerly a truck

**Above:** *Chouteau County Free Library, Montana's first Carnegie Library*

1918. The Women's Club is instrumental in the ongoing care of the library; the McLeish family was financially responsible for the 1992 addition.

The rush for land provided Fort Benton with a different kind of boom. The influx of people crowded existing housing in the community. A new story on the Choteau House and residents taking in boarders helped alleviate the problem.

On the corner of Front and

**Top right:** *T.C. Power Lumber Company was built to compete with the Missouri River Lumber Company.*

**Right:** *With the influx of boarders during the Homestead Era, Jere Sullivan added a third story to the Choteau House to capture some of the prosperity.*

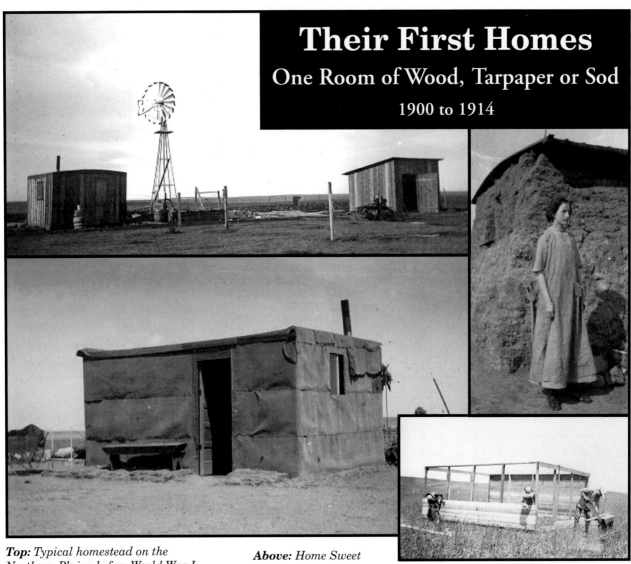

# Their First Homes
## One Room of Wood, Tarpaper or Sod
### 1900 to 1914

*Top:* Typical homestead on the
Northern Plains before World War I

*Above:* Home Sweet
Home, all in tarpaper

*Above:* Building on the prairie

*Top above:* "Soddies" were
warm but maintenance was
horrendous!

*Left:* Some women took up
a homestead by themselves.

*Below:* A few could
afford more . . .

*Above:* In winter it was tough
to keep from freezing to death.

*Left:* An
entire
family
lived in
only one
room.

*Top: Levee in 1910 with T.C. Power & Bro. and H.J. Wackerlin Hardware*

*Above: Ah Sing was a laundryman, one of many local Chinese businessmen.*

*Right: City Shop, run by Emil Breault, was one of the fast-disappearing institutions in Fort Benton's business district*

garden operated by Japanese residents and abandoned when the Oriental population left Fort Benton.

## Chinese

In its early years Fort Benton was a very tolerant community with regard to minorities, except the Native Americans. The Chinese started businesses during the gold rush days of the 1860's, but only three appeared in the 1870 census, all washermen. The 1880 census listed nine as cooks and in the laundry trade. Newspapers mentioned several Chinese working at ranches as houseboys and cooks.

The local Orientals moved into old buildings in the block just below the old bridge, once the "Bloodiest Block in the West," and established laundries, restaurants, saloons and shops selling mercantile goods particularly imported silk. Even opium dens crept into a

144

*Above:* Completing Power Motors, one of three new garages built for the automobile

*Top left:* Built in 1928, Central Service Station was Fort Benton's first; owners were John Lepley and Lee Preuninger.

few of the basements, and were not only patronized by the Chinese! By 1900 there were thirty Chinese on the census rolls.

Great Falls had passed an exclusion act, and discrimination soon reared its ugly head in Fort Benton also. In 1923 the cook at the Quan Cafe hanged himself, the manager and staff closed the establishment and left the same day for Lethbridge, Alberta. The Chinese population was absent for many years.

## From Horses to Cars

The blacksmith shop and livery gave way to garages and service stations for automobiles. H. LaBarre built a new brick garage and moved the old blacksmith shop to the back lot in 1915. Power followed suit and built Power Motors, and Theis and Patterson built another garage on Front Street. In 1928 Lepley and Preuninger built Central Service, Fort Benton's first service station. Cars and trucks replaced horses and wagons on the city streets, and road building became a major chore in Chouteau County.

During the early years of World War I, Fort Benton experi-

enced three great years of prosperity (1914-1916) with high farm prices and an influx of people. The town was rated as the richest per capita in the nation with $1600 for every man, woman and child.

The only disaster during those years occurred when the T.C. Power and Bro. store was destroyed by fire. The new flour mill built in 1914 ran at full capacity and six blocks of Front Street were paved. The school had grown so large with children of homesteaders that a new wing was added in 1916, almost equal in floor space to the 1884 building.

Horses were sold on the average at $180 a head. Elevators in Big Sandy were plugged; there were 300 wagons waiting in line to unload! Just before it all changed

*Below:* In 1915 the Treasure State Band played in front of T.C. Power & Bro.'s store. It seems that Fort Benton always has had a City Band.

*Above: Mullan Road Memorial dedicated in 1917, Fort Benton's first monument and the first such marker in Montana*

*Top right: Construction of the 1916 addition to the school in progress*

*Below: Completed addition to high school during the homestead period*

once again, Fort Benton dedicated the first Mullan Trail Monument; Governor Stewart unveiled it in September 1917.

## The Bust

As war clouds continued to gather in 1917, rain clouds disappeared over Montana. It was not until the U.S. entered the war that the new farmers finally felt the wrath of Montana weather. Drought hit hard; no one ever imagined that these high plains could be so dry.

With America's entry into the war, the Federal government pegged the wheat price per bushel at $2.20. Such financial encouragement prompted farmers to produce more wheat. They borrowed on easy credit to expand their farming operations. During the spring of 1917 more and more acres of sod were broken up for seeding, and farmers went deeper and deeper into debt. Then the drought set in. The end of the war in 1918 brought a decline in farm prices worldwide and an instant

# Big Farms and Big Machines
## Encouraged by World War I

*Left:* Threshing grain with a steam traction engine and a separator

*Below:* Cutting grain with 32 mules and a wooden combine on the Ed Kelly ranch

*Left:* Steam traction engine hauling eight wagons of grain to market, at about four miles an hour!

*Below left:* Breaking sod to increase acreage during World War I

*Below:* Filling a new granary even before it's completed

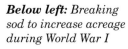

**Above right:** *Dedication of the World War I Memorial, "Spirit of the American Doughboy," in 1922*

depression occurred across the Northern Plains. Over 60,000 people had left Montana by 1921.

**Above:** *"The Doughboy" Memorial on Front Street was the first war memorial in Montana.*

## Patriotism and The Great War

By war's end Montana had furnished the largest proportion per population to the armed forces . . . and had the highest casualty rate. Chouteau County ranked number one in both statistics within the state; 73 were killed in action during the Great War. Henry W. Griesbach Jr. was the first resident to perish while serving with the Canadians.

The home front supported her boys overseas. Montanans purchased more Liberty Bonds per capita than any other state. Chouteau County ranked first in Montana through five drives totalling $2,441,400. When Armistice Day arrived, 1231 had been inducted into the armed forces from Chouteau County and 512 volunteers had served during the war.

## Post-War Years

The weather remained hot and dry. 1919 was the driest in forty years, and the exodus from

**Right:** *Patriotic parade after World War I. Chouteau County provided more service personnel per capita than any county in the nation.*

*Left: Bartley's Livery, one of many businesses that were lost when the country changed from horses to automobiles*

the farms and out of Montana continued. Prohibition dried things further in 1920. In Fort Benton the bottle only moved to the back room, and activities carried on much as they had during the days of the fur trade when illegal whiskey flowed like water. After forty years, on January 1, 1920 Fort Benton lost its daily newspaper, but the *River Press* continues as a weekly publication to the present.

In 1921 the obstinate Great Northern Railroad finally agreed to change the name of the station to Fort Benton rather than just Benton, after local residents had complained since 1887. For the first time in five years the weather improved and crops were better.

The *U.S.S. Mandan* appeared at the Fort Benton levee in 1922, the last steamboat to reach Fort Benton.

Grasshoppers infested the crops that year, and farmland was worth less than what had been borrowed against it. Banks closed all over the state; the Benton State Bank closed its doors in December 1922. The Stockman's National Bank failed in January 1924; the stockholders paid off 97 cents on the dollar to its creditors. Some say the bank should never have closed! In April the bank from Square Butte was brought to town and became the Chouteau County Bank.

The town was saddened by the death of its illustrious citizen, Thomas C. Power, on March 16, 1923. He had come to Fort Benton in 1867, developed one of Montana's largest mercantile empires and went on to become a U.S. Senator.

*Below: Fort Benton loves a parade. The Fort Benton Band led the parade down Front Street after the turn-of-the-century.*

*Right:* Benton State Bank just before the Montana closures 1922-1924

On November 11, 1923 Chouteau County was the first in Montana to dedicate "The Spirit of the American Doughboy," a memorial to its World War I dead. Completion of the project was due to the tireless efforts of W. K. Harber, editor of the *River Press*, and D.G. Browne, President of the Stockmen's National Bank. Unfortunately, both had passed away before the dedication.

## Recovery

*Below:* Mandan's last trip to Fort Benton in 1921

By 1926 recovery was at hand. In July the Montana Pioneers met in Fort Benton, the first big celebration of many. Fort Benton friends mourned the pass-

ing of Charles M. Russell, a frequent visitor, in October.

The county produced over 5 million bushels of wheat in 1928 and became Montana's premier grain producer, a position it re-

*Above: Sons and Daughters on Front Street after the parade*

*Left: Everyone adjourned to the "water hole" and left their horses at the hitching post.*

tains to the present. As a coincidence, Fort Benton's only flour mill burned to the ground that same year.

The State Legislature designated Fort Benton as the site for the State Memorial to Lewis

*Left: Henry Lyon's bronze of Lewis and Clark, taken from C.M. Russell's drawings, for the State Memorial in Fort Benton*

and Clark but provided no appropriations. The stock market crash in 1929 led the nation into economic chaos. With Montana headed into the Great Depression, the project was forgotten until the Bicentennial in 1976.

*Far left: One of Charlie's last visits to Old Fort Benton before his passing in 1926*

151

# Carter, Montana
## Typical Homestead Town

*Above:* The schoolhouse shows what great expectations homesteaders had for their new town.

*Above left:* Earl and Tate, general merchandise store in the center of town

*Above right:* A.H. Stewart's Livery and St. Anthony and Dakota Lumber Co. at the end of Main Street

*Right:* Main Street businesses were wood-frame establishments.

*Left:* Main Street ran parallel to the Great Northern tracks. It was four blocks long in 1912.

152

*Chapter 9*

# Depression and War, 1929-1945

*The stock market crash forced the nation into a deep depression that ended with the New Deal of the Roosevelt Administration and the Second World War.*

## Natural Disasters

The stock market crash of 1929 brought on the Great Depression and across America everyone tightened their belts. To make matters worse, drought caused crop failure in the West. Hordes of insects and dust clouds turned day into night. People who lived through those times never forgot, and even today demonstrate some habits in their daily living acquired during those years.

*Above: When the wool warehouse was torn down, Baker Company records were lost.*

## Depression Brought Change

The nation looked for a change . . . out with the old and in with the new. The trend was to light colors and to streamline everything from cars to trains to architecture. Houses and commercial buildings suffered when owners made changes that left only a muddled mess that neither looked good nor was practical, but it was Change!

Fort Benton was no different. In 1929 the Masons bought the Benton Record Building and tore off

*Left: Remodeled Benton Record Building after removal of the third story and its Victorian splendor. Only a plain yellow cube remained as the Masonic Hall.*

153

*Right: The school burning in the August 1936 fire, and the fire's aftermath*

the third story. In the process the glass negatives of Dan Dutro were destroyed; Dutro had been a photographer in Fort Benton, recording its history from the 1870's through the 1890's. The trim was removed, the building was stuccoed and painted a cream color. It resembled an ugly yellow cube!

To build a new swimming pool, the WPA demolished the old wool warehouse. With it went all records of the largest mercantile business in Montana, the I.G. Baker Company. An attempt to create a museum during those years failed for lack of interest and money. In the meantime, the school burned and its large case of historic artifacts was lost.

Charlie Bovey committed the final insult. He bought and moved Jos. Sullivan's Saddlery to Old Town in Great Falls. It probably would have been torn down if it had remained in Fort Benton. The Boveys were among the few who were interested in saving Montana's heritage at that time. Although Old Town did not survive, the saddlery was saved and is in Nevada City today.

*Right: Front Street - Chouteau County Bank, Benton Drug Store, Pool Hall, Gamble Store and Louther Mortuary*

## Hard Times

By 1930 roads were under construction all across the county. A new one was built between Great Falls and Fort Benton; graveling was finished in 1930 and it was oiled two years later.

From 1920 to 1930 Chouteau County's population fell from 10,450 to 8,600, but Fort Benton's grew from 1065 to 1110. In 1932 the American Legion built Memorial Park, a triangular-shaped green next to Old Fort Park between Front and Main Streets. Crops in the county were good in 1932 but prices had dropped to a new national low.

In April 1932 people were dancing in the streets for prohibition was over. Whiskey and beer came out of the back rooms and "speak easys" became legal.

The old giant T.C. Power and Bro. declared bankruptcy in 1934. A group of local citizens formed a corporation and purchased the big store, renaming it Pioneer Mercantile Co. The hardware was bought by Frank Palmer, a manager for Powers, and the garage was sold to N.S. Swanson.

After the election of Franklin D. Roosevelt, the Federal government's "alphabet agencies"

*Below:* *The swimming pool, built by the WPA in 1936-1937, resembled the old fort.*

# *The Last Department Store*
# Liquidation of T.C. Power & Bro.
## 1867 - 1934

***Right:*** *Women's notions and clothing on the main floor*

***Above:*** *The drygoods department was upstairs in the building across the street.*

***Right:*** *Furniture in the basement*

***Below right:*** *Music department upstairs*

***Below:*** *Groceries on the main floor*

***Above:*** *Shoes and men's department on the main floor*

*Right:* T.C. Power & Bro. went bankrupt in 1934. Their store in Fort Benton was purchased by local interests in 1932 who renamed it the Pioneer Mercantile.

## Low Prices, Drought and Insects

*Left:* Grasshoppers covered everything; it looked as if the whole landscape were moving.

Farmers were still deep in the Depression in 1935. They not only were faced with low prices, but also Mormon crickets and army worms arrived to make things worse.

An earthquake shook the area that year, toppling so many bricks off the chimneys of the Grand Union that they all had to be removed. Helena was devastated by the quake; Fort Benton raised relief funds to help in their plight.

*Below:* Building county roads was a big job in such a large county with so many miles to cover.

came to town. There was the NRA, CCC, WPA and in October 1200 farmers signed up for the allotment called the AAA. The single biggest Federal project to help Montanans was construction of Fort Peck Dam on the Missouri River, the biggest earth-filled dam in the world at that time. It provided jobs that helped dig the state's economy from the depths of despair, and gave eastern Montana residents a sense of well-being again.

**Right:** *Conductor Ed Shields and Agent Tony Schanche with Shep*

**Below:** *Shep, Forever Faithful*

**Below:** *Shep on the platform, waiting for his master's return*

In December the Old West returned. Bandits broke into four Fort Benton businesses, pocketed 35 pennies and made off in a stolen car. (There really was a Depression!). Two days later the thieves were caught red-handed in Shelby. After the gunsmoke cleared, two law officers and one banditto lay dead. The rest were behind bars by nightfall.

When there was little else to talk about, there was always the weather. On February 3, 1936 it warmed up to 2 below zero. The next day the bottom fell out of the thermometer when it dropped to 42 below, and that is where stayed until Feb. 17. When an old-timer says "Remember the winter of . . .", it really did get that cold.

## Shep, Forever Faithful

In the fall of 1936 a scraggly old shepherd dog showed up at the railroad depot. He met all passenger trains that came to the station then disappeared under the platform. It was not until the next year that Great Northern Conductor Ed

Shields pieced together the dog's story. Affectionately named Shep, his vigil lasted seven years. Hoping against hope that his dead master would return, Shep never missed a train until, old and hard of hearing, he was hit by a train. After a funeral attended by 200 mourners, Shep was buried on the hill above the depot.

## Boat Race

Construction of Fort Peck Dam triggered a celebration in Fort Benton. Boats in the St. Louis to Fort Benton Boat Race were the last up the free-flowing river before the dam closed it forever. On the final day, the cruiser *Fort Benton* lead the pack under the bridge with 10,000 people lining the levee. It was a spectacular celebration at the Head of Navigation on the Missouri River.

During the celebration, the mountain howitzer stationed in Fort Benton during the Indian Wars of 1876-1877 was returned by the City of Great Falls where it had been taken many years before.

The first municipal water system in Montana was aging and needed replacing. A new brick water treatment plant with settling basins was built. Construction also began on a new two-story elementary school with gymnasium. It was

*Above: Mayor Bowker (to right of flag pole) accepting cannon returned by Great Falls during 1937 boat race*

*Below: New high school was completed in 1938 after fire destroyed the old building.*

# St. Louis to Fort Benton Boat Race

**Blackfoot Indians from Browning helped celebrate the last boats upriver from St. Louis, commemorating their role in the history of the river and Fort Benton.**

*Above: Fort Benton's crew: Mayor Roy Bowker, Al Jones, Capt. Lee Preuninger*

***Top:*** *Cruiser Fort Benton crossing the finish line under the old bridge while a crowd of some 10,000 looked on*

***Above:*** *Blackfoot dancers performing at the fairgrounds*

***Above right:*** *Chris-craft cruisers tied up at the dock: Great Falls, Fort Benton, Malta and Glasgow-Fort Peck. The race was won by the boat from Glasgow-Fort Peck.*

***Right:*** *Blackfoot band in native dress*

160

# June 18-20, 1937
# Celebration

*Left: Blackfoot Indians parading down Front Street in their finest regalia*

*Above: Blackfoot Indians on horseback during the parade*

*Above: Boy Scout Bike Patrol: leader Chet Overholser; Scouts Dick Moses, Clark Hilton, Bill Louther and Ken Vinion*

*Right: Blackfoot village of colorful teepees at the fairgrounds*

*Above: First contingent of Chouteau County boys going off to World War II*

*Right: U.S. Judge Charles N. Pray served many illustrious years on the bench and was one of Fort Benton's foremost citizens after his years in Congress.*

*Below: Do you remember 1936? Temperatures were below -25° for several weeks. The river froze deep and ice piled up, nearly taking out the old bridge, but finally went out without flooding.*

finished just in time; on August 2 the old 1884 building and its addition caught fire and burned to the ground. School started late that year! Classes were held in many places in town until the mess was cleaned up and a new high school was built the next year. Despite the turmoil, in 1937 the school graduated a record 51 seniors and placed third in the state in the scholarship contest.

## Crickets and Nazis

Mormon crickets and grasshoppers showed up again with a vengeance. The whole county mustered to fight them off with ditches, pits and waste oil pools. When crossing the roads, the hordes of insects made highways as slippery as driving on ice. They devastated the fields as they scoured the countryside. 1938 brought rains, floods and good crops, but low prices forced farmers to store grain in anything they could find.

Again the world was at war when the Germans invaded Poland. In Fort Benton the new Christian Church was finished after parishoners had held services in a basement for years.

At the beginning of 1940 the census in Chouteau County had dropped to 7,316, but Fort Benton's had increased to 1227 residents. The first peacetime draft in October took the first Chouteau County men, and many volunteered for military service.

## "A Date Which Will Live In Infamy"
President Franklin D. Roosevelt

Isolationists tried to keep America out of the fray, but when the Japanese attacked Pearl Harbor on December 7, the U.S. went to war. Chouteau County gave up her first dead. Emil O. Ronning was wounded

*Left: 1939 businesses - Zoller Chevrolet, River Press and Davis Bros. Store; notice the old street lights.*

that morning and died several days later. Other local men were wounded at Pearl and in the Philippines that day.

The next four years of war brought many changes. Detachment after detachment marched off to war, leaving mothers and sisters to man the farm machinery, store counters, and gasoline pumps. Gold Star banners appeared in the windows of Chouteau County homes. They were years of sacrifice. Tires, gasoline, meat, sugar and canned goods were rationed. Everyone saved grease, aluminum, scrap iron and newspapers for collection drives held throughout the war years. Every month brought new casualty lists. D-Day on June 6, 1944 gave hope that it might soon be over.

Again Montana led the nation in War Bond sales per capita, and Chouteau County was first in the state. By war's end Chouteau County had purchased $774 in bonds for every man, woman and child in the county.

## Soldiers Return to the Old Fort

In an unusual turn of events in 1943, Fort Benton again became a military post. The fort was closed in 1881 and the military reservation

was sold to the public. Some say the military looked at a map and saw the "fort" designation, not realizing that the military reservation had been sold! For whatever reason, on July 26 the 331st Service Group of the U.S. Army Air Force arrived by train. Eventually its 1100 men were to be shipped to England. Troop movements were backed up, and men needed temporary quarters until space was available to send them overseas. It was the high point of the war for Bentonites. They had the heartwarming task of caring for those Air Force Angels who were received with open arms. For over a month residents couldn't do enough for those boys who were defending our country.

*Below: Chouteau County soldiers at Fort Knox. Back row: Bob Ray, Francis Willis, William Larson, Fred McKenzie, Charles Geiser; middle row: Laddie Nepil, John Wolf, Alvis Vestal, Elmer Dostal, John Balazic; front row: Gus Jappe, Ralph Rowland, Charles Knudson, Clarence O'Neil, Claude Hansen, Harold McKerrow*

*Right:* Front Street in the 1930's with the Louther Mortuary and Scarlet's Gamble Store

*Below:* Built in 1881 as the Centennial Hotel, the name was first changed to the Pacific Hotel, then to the Culbertson House and by the 1930's it was called the Casey Block.

Officers were quartered in homes around town much as they had been during the 1870's. Tents were set up at the fairgrounds for the enlisted men. A USO was opened in the old I.G. Baker store, men were invited to dinner in local homes, and some budding romances developed. Dinner guests sometimes "smuggled" sugar from camp to replace rationed sugar used in cakes and pies! Dances, theater productions and concerts were held. Little or no trouble occurred during their stay and it was a glorious time.

By September the troops were on their way to Europe, with fond memories of the little river town that had given its heart to them. The townsfolk had newly-adopted sons to write to, and to worry about until war's end.

## Bumper Harvest

The weather cooperated during the war years. With help from young boys, girls and women, farmers raised bumper crops to feed those overseas. In 1944 and 1945 an extra million acres of wheat had been planted, and there was not enough equipment to harvest the enormous crop. The government stepped in and allowed Massey-Harris to stop tank production and produce 500 self-propelled combines each year to cut the crop. The Harvest Brigade began in Texas and moved slowly north to Montana and North Dakota, following the ripening grain. It was one of the biggest successful home front stories of World War II, and the beginning of custom combining that continues today.

## The War's Over

On August 14, 1945 the Japanese surrendered and there was again dancing in the streets. Every-one eagerly awaited the return of their sons and daughters, but demobilization took time. A point system was used to determine who were sent home first. U.S. industry needed a year or two to convert into the post-war economy. Most home front equipment was just about worn out after four years of war and needed replacing.

Fort Benton was ready to enter the post-war period. With an up-beat economy, good prices and good crops, the river port began its second one hundred years as the Birthplace of Montana.

# Changing Times

*Right: Towner Boys' Band of the 1920's and 1930's, one of several community bands organized during Fort Benton's history*

*Right: The river still jams in the winter, and everyone watches closely until it goes out.*

*Right: Montana's first municipal water plant was replaced in 1934 by a modern treatment facility with settling basins on the side.*

*Right: In 1939 the First Christian Church was built over the basement that had been in use since 1916.*

*Chapter 10*

# Post-War Era

*It was a time of state-wide celebrations and a reminder of the storied past of the Birthplace of Montana. Fort Benton's acclaimed national Bicentennial effort was Montana's Memorial to Lewis and Clark.*

## Coming Home

The war was over in 1946 and the service men and women returned home. The region bloomed into an era of prosperity. The area's diversity in agriculture changed decidedly after World War II as it had during the first World War. 86% of Montana's agricultural economy was invested in three products: wheat, barley and cattle. Chouteau County was a mirror image of the state. The county remained the largest wheat producer in the state and among the top ten nationally. It also enjoyed the highest per capita income in the country.

The rains came. With a favorable post-war market price for wheat, the economy soared. Arrival of electricity in rural areas and replacement of household goods after the war produced a boom for retail merchants. Items that were worn out or rationed were in production as American industry geared up for the peace time economy. Coming on the market were the answers to everyone's dreams; some waited a year for that new car or refrigerator! It was an era of optimism, in the midst of which Fort Benton celebrated her first hundred years.

*Below: Fort Benton in 1939. The town changed little through the war years.*

# 100th Birthday

*Right:* Logo of the 1946 Centennial Celebration

The gala event was held on August 24 and 25. It attracted thousands from all over the state and throughout the nation who came honor the oldest continuous white settlement in Montana and its birthplace.

The Blackfoot returned to their premier trading post and first agency, and helped celebrate their history during Fort Benton's fur trade era. A large village was set up next to the high bluffs where their ancestors had camped one hundred years earlier.

There were giant parades with stagecoaches, long bull trains, bands, vintage automobiles, horses and riders. Dressed in their ceremonial clothing, the Blackfoot paraded and danced. Dignitaries recognized the city's role with eloquent speeches, and the Governor addressed the large crowds on the last day. The honored guest was Admiral John H. Hoover, Deputy Commander in the Pacific during World War II.

During two evenings a spectacular outdoor historical pageant was staged. The pageant emphasized the Native Americans and historical figures of Fort Benton's and Montana's history, and the importance of the town in river trade and opening of the Northwest. Everyone had a marvelous time. It must have been like the old Fourth of July celebrations of the 1860's only with far less gun play and fist fights!

There was a sad note to the grand occasion. One of the last remaining adobe walls of the original fort toppled over the day before the festivities. Perhaps its end signaled the finale of the first hundred years.

The St. Louis to Fort Benton Boat Race of 1937 and the 1946 Centennial triggered a series of celebrations. There were festivals in 1954, 1960, 1964, and 1969. The whole state was invited to enjoy the pageantry of Tall Tales of Fort Benton, the First Steamboat Arrival, Territorial Status for Montana, and the Beginning of the Whoop-Up Trail. Those festivities preceded the biggest one of all, the celebration of America's Bicentennial in 1976 and the dedication of the State of Montana's Memorial to Lewis and Clark.

*Below:* 1946 Centennial Planning Committee meeting in the Grand Union. L to R: H.F. Miller, Monte Lockwood, Chairman; John T. Lepley, Vice Chairman; Katherine Wackerlin, Secretary; Carl Shogren, Frank Morger, Wes Cloyd

# 1946 Fort Benton Centennial

*Above: Blackfoot Elders*

*Above: Entire cast in the finale of the Centennial pageant*

*Above: Two scenes from the pageant: fur trade at the fort and the arrival of the first steamboat to Fort Benton*

*Above: Six-oxen team wagon hitch, stagecoach in background. Joe Marion, bullwhacker, on horseback; Les Baldwin and Joe Beard*

*Three views of the Centennial Parade*

*Left: Blackfoot performing native dances on Front Street*

## History Lost

*Above:* 1949 fire destroyed the Overland Hotel and several other historic business buildings.

In 1949 the most serious fire in the history of the Front Street business district destroyed a half dozen old buildings between 12th and 13th Streets. The Overland Hotel was a major historic loss. New structures uncharacteristic of the historic district were built in their stead. A few years later the 1881 two-story brick building housing the drug store and doctor's office collapsed from old age and soft bricks. Structures constructed of soft brick in the 1880's are endangered today if not cared for properly.

*Above and Right:* 1955 collapse of the Lockwood building, rebuilt as Larson's Drug Store

*Above: William Johnstone: Superintendent of Schools, founder of the Community Improvement Association and museum builder*

In 1953 after heavy June rains, the Missouri lapped at the levee again. Highwood Creek ravaged its entire valley, floating homes off their foundations, removing bridges and roads with ease and changing its course in many places.

## New History Museum and the CIA

The few display cases of artifacts burned with the school in 1936; an attempt to create a museum in 1936-1937 failed. Fort Benton finally constructed a modern museum in 1956-1957, one of the first community institutions of its kind in the state.

The Fort Benton Community Improvement Association was established in 1956 by Wm. Johnstone. Under his guidance and CIA sponsorship, the Fort Benton Museum was built. It was a community effort, with many people lending their talents to bring about its completion. In 1965 a major addition was constructed by Hugh Simmons and Bob Leinart. Its name was changed to the Museum of the Upper Missouri when the exhibits assumed a more regional nature.

The museum depicts the area's early beginnings, from prehistory to statehood and the turn-of-the-19th century. It exhibits some priceless artifacts including

*Top left: Old bridge in the June flood of 1953. The river reached the top of the levee but didn't run over.*

*Below: Fort Benton Museum completed in 1957 Inset: The museum of 1936 was never completed in the old Kleinschmidt Warehouse.*

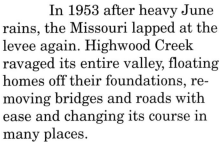

# The Golden Triangle

## Montana's Largest Wheat Producing Area

**Chouteau County is Montana's largest wheat producer**

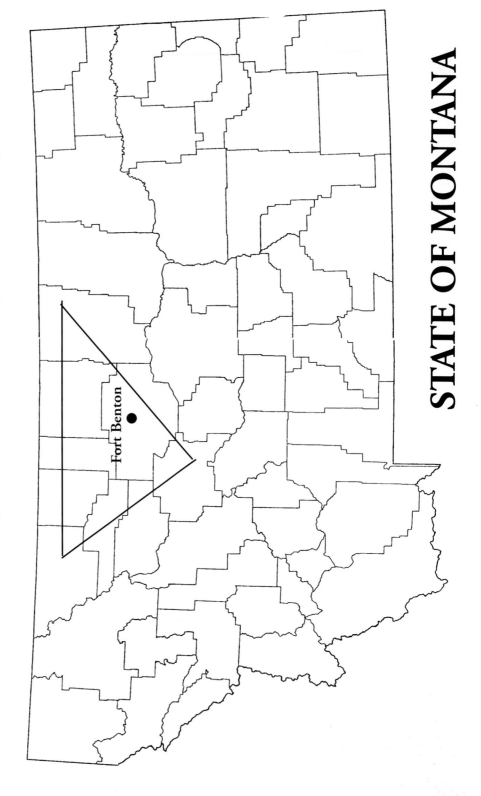

**STATE OF MONTANA**

Chief Joseph's surrender rifle, the mountain howitzer from the Nez Perce War, and the log of the steamer *Benton*. Also on display are Juneau's cabin, an 1880 hearse, the Block P that hung between the stacks of the steamboat *Butte*, and a collection of artifacts from Montana's first military fort at Camp Cooke.

In 1956 Fort Benton put an end to its muddy streets. A special improvement district covering most of the town instigated new curbing and gutters; paved streets were finished that summer. In the next year Fort Benton's worst tragedy occurred. Five students and their music teacher were killed on their way to a music festival. Their deaths touched almost everyone in town.

School enrollment grew when the post-war baby boomers reached high school age. A new high school was completed in 1958 on the old baseball diamond to accommodate projected record enrollments in the 1970's. The Sisters of Charity built a new hospital which they operated until 1975 when they left Fort Benton, after serving the community for ninety years.

# New Bridge Across the Missouri

The old bridge was closed in 1963 after serving this area of Montana since 1887. The old spans could no longer accommodate two-way traffic and trucks carrying bigger loads were stressing her trusses. There was still a life for her; in 1980 she was reopened as a walking bridge, saving Montana's most historic bridge.

The new bridge opened in 1963. Both bridges were tested by the flood waters of 1964. For the new bridge it was the first test,

*Above: Fort Benton Senior High School completed in 1958*

*Below: New hospital built in 1952 by the Sisters of Charity*

*Above: Chouteau County Bridge built at Fort Benton in 1963, during the high water of the 1964 flood.*

## National Historic Landmark

and the old lady survived yet another. Rapid, heavy snow melt and torrential June rains swelled the Missouri and streams along the eastern front of the Rockies to above flood stage. Every town in their path, including Fort Benton, was endangered by rising water. Unlike 1908, the Missouri River dams held and helped control the flow, but along the Teton, Sun and Two Medicine people lost loved ones, livestock, homes and crops. Fort Benton was lucky. The water lapped at the top of the levee but never ran over.

In 1965 Fort Benton received National Historic Landmark status in recognition of its national importance to Western Expansion. Landmark status was accorded to the fort site and the steamboat levee, and recognized a historical district within the city.

NBC came in 1965 to film a documentary related to the journey of Lewis and Clark. The company borrowed the keelboat *Mandan*, built for the movie "Big Sky," for their production. The Montana Historical Society left the boat for display on the levee rather than return it to the weed-covered back lot in Helena.

*Right: Debris at the Loma bridges after a flood of the Teton and Marias River Valleys*

## 125 Years and Fort Benton's Top Brass

In September 1971 the people of Fort Benton celebrated their Quasquicentennial (125th anniversary). Some of her most distinguished sons, who had risen to Flag rank in the service of our country, were guests of honor.

In the late 1920's there were several young men who graduated from Chouteau County High School in Fort Benton who went on to pursue careers in the U.S. military. In 1923-1924 there were four midshipmen at Annapolis and one cadet at West Point from Fort Benton. Those young men were inspired and encouraged by a very special principal and math teacher, Cleveland M. Luce, and by John H. Hoover USN who had preceded them to the naval academy.

After graduation from the respective academies, they became career officers in the armed forces. Pearl Harbor found them at various posts and ships, serving as junior officers in many far-flung bases. They attained rank rapidly in combat, and by the end of the conflict were high-ranking officers. All served brilliantly during World War II and, with the many contingents from Fort Benton, became hometown heroes.

One was lost in the Pacific. On April 3, 1943 Lt. Commander Thomas F. Sharp was lost on a combat patrol in Japanese waters aboard the submarine *USS Pickerel.* Although his ultimate potential was never realized, classmates at the academy remember him as cut from the same cloth as the

*Above:* USS Pickerel, fleet submarine that was lost with Commander Sharp on board

*Above: Lt. Commander Thomas Sharp was lost on war patrol in 1943 off Honshu aboard the submarine USS Pickerel.*

others and surely destined to become an admiral. The other favorite sons obtained Flag rank in their respective branches of the military and served illustrious careers before retirement.

There are seven distinguished Flag Officers who graduated from Fort Benton, quite an accomplishment for a small town of less than 2000! Her citizens embrace them as their own, and are extremely proud of the honor they have brought to their community. There are two four-star Admirals, one Vice Admiral, one Rear Admiral, one Major General in the Army and two Brigadier Generals, one in the U.S. Marines and one in the U.S. Air Force.

# Admiral John Howard Hoover

John Hoover started the parade of Fort Benton youth who went to the academies and on to illustrious military careers. He

*Right: Fleet Admiral Chester W. Nimitz, Commander of the Pacific Theater, with Admiral John H. Hoover, Deputy Commander of the Pacific*

# Fort Benton's Four-Star Admirals

*Left: Four-star Admiral U.S. Grant Sharp, Commander of the Pacific 1964-1968*

*Below: Four-star Admiral John H. Hoover, Deputy Commander of the Pacific 1944-1946 and later Commander of Navy Air on the Pacific coast*

was born in Seville, Ohio on May 15, 1887, and came to Fort Benton with his widowed mother Claudia, a school teacher. After finishing the eighth grade in Fort Benton, he attended high school in Great Falls since there was no high school in Fort Benton. Hoover graduated from the Naval Academy in 1907, served with a destroyer force in Ireland during World War I, and was awarded the Navy Cross.

In the interim years between wars he saw submarine service and became a naval aviator. World War II found Hoover a Rear Admiral and Commander of the Caribbean. In 1943 he became Commander of Carrier Division 4 of the Pacific Fleet. Later he was Commander of the Air Arm of the

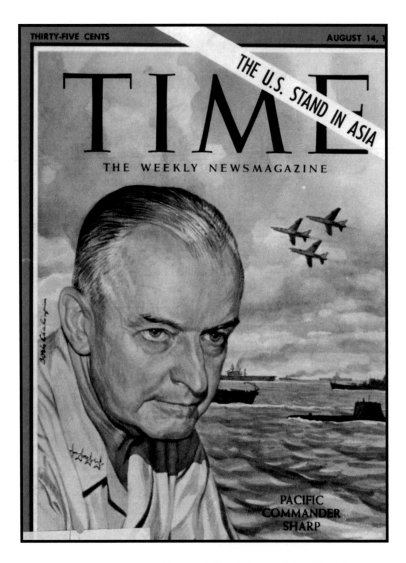

THIRTY-FIVE CENTS                                    AUGUST 14, 1

# TIME
## THE WEEKLY NEWSMAGAZINE

THE U.S. STAND IN ASIA

PACIFIC
COMMANDER
SHARP

*Above: Time magazine's cover August 14, 1964 just after Admiral Sharp took Command of the Pacific*

Central Pacific, and in 1945 he became Deputy Commander and Chief of the Pacific Fleet next to Fleet Admiral Chester Nimitz. After the war Admiral Hoover was Commander of Fleet Air on the west coast and served in Washington D.C. until his retirement in 1948 as a four-star Admiral.

## Admiral U.S. Grant Sharp

Grant Sharp was born in Chinook, Montana on April 2, 1906, and came to Fort Benton with his parents where he started the first grade. He graduated from the Naval Academy in 1927 and served at many stations and on many ships before World War II.

Sharp was Commander of the destroyer *USS Hogan* on convoy duty in the North Atlantic and in the invasion of North Africa. He was transferred to the Pacific where he commanded the destroyer *USS Boyd* during the island-hopping campaign and the Battle of the Philippine Sea. He was awarded two Silver Stars for gallantry in that action.

Following World War II, Sharp was a staff officer in the Pacific Fleet and planned the Inchon Landing while commanding Destroyer Squadron Five. As Chief of Staff Pacific Fleet, in 1955 he was promoted to Rear Admiral. After several other commands Admiral Sharp became Commander of the U.S. First Fleet and promoted to Vice Admiral. He served an important planning role in the Cuban Missile Crisis as Deputy Chief of Naval Operations in Washington.

In 1963 he was promoted to full Admiral and three days later became Commander-in-Chief of the Pacific Fleet, the world's largest naval command. On June 30, 1964, Admiral Sharp became Commander of all armed services in the Pacific. His responsibilities included over a million men, 600 major ships and 8000 aircraft, all involved in the Vietnam War from 1964 to 1968. Two gold stars and a second Distinguished Service Medal accompanied his retirement in 1968.

178

## Vice Admiral George Crosby Towner

Born in Fort Benton on March 19, 1901, George Towner graduated from the local high school in 1919. Following graduation from the Naval Academy, he served on several ships: *USS New Mexico*, *USS Vestal* and the carrier *USS Saratoga*. He was aboard the cruiser *USS Louisville* in the South Pacific when the Japanese attacked Pearl Harbor. In 1944 after his tour on the *Louisville* Towner took command of the *USS Yosemite*, a destroyer tender. Towner's proudest command was in 1948, the *USS Helena*, named for the capitol of his home state. He was promoted to Rear Admiral and given command of the service forces for the Sixth Fleet, and was later Commander of the Middle East Forces. Towner's promotion to Vice Admiral occurred in 1958 when he became Commander of the Amphibious Forces of the Atlantic Fleet. His last command was the 13th Naval District in Seattle. Admiral Towner retired from active duty on March 30, 1963.

## Rear Admiral Louis Dent Sharp

Louis Sharp was born on March 17, 1901 in Fort Benton, just two days before his life-long friend and roommate at the Naval Academy, Admiral George Towner. After his commission Sharp served

*Left: Vice Admiral George C. Towner, Commander of U.S. Amphibious Forces*

aboard the *USS Texas* and on several destroyers in the Pacific, some on Yangtze River patrol in China. At the onset of World War II Sharp was aboard the *USS New Mexico*. After serving the Navy Department in Washington, in 1944 he received command of his own ship, the attack transport *USS Goodhue*. Sharp was commended following a kamikaze attack on his ship at Okinawa. In the Korean War he was Task Group Commander for the Inchon Landing. Sharp was Commanding Officer of the naval amphibious

*Below: USS Pocono, Admiral Towner's flagship when he was Commander of the Amphibious Forces Atlantic Fleet*

179

*Right:* *Rear Admiral Louis Dent Sharp, USN*

Officer of the naval amphibious forces at Coronado, California and in 1951 was promoted to Rear Admiral based upon his combat awards. Admiral Sharp retired in 1954.

# Major General Raymond Wiley Curtis

*Below: As a young officer, General Curtis competed in the Olympics for the United States*

Born in Helena on February 22, 1904 Ray Curtis completed all of his schooling in Fort Benton and graduated in 1921. He graduated

*Above: Major General Raymond C. Curtis, U.S. Army*

from West Point in 1927 and served with the cavalry. Curtis was one of its finest equestrians, a member of two national riding teams that competed in the Olympics.

Curtis rose rapidly in various commands after 1941. In 1943 he was Assistant Chief of Staff of the Fifth Army in Italy. He was awarded the Silver Star when he captured German prisoners during a stint on the front lines. After the war Curtis commanded the Third Armored Mechanized Cavalry and in 1950 he was Commander of the Third Armored at Fort Knox. Curtis returned to Europe in 1952 and received his Brigadier General's Star as Commander of the 14th Armored Cavalry. He returned to Fort Knox as Assistant Commander of the armor school, and was named Chief of the Joint Command in Korea. Curtis was promoted to Major General in 1958. He was Commander of the II Corps at Camp Kilmer before he retired on June 30, 1961.

180

## Brigadier General Karl Kreuger Louther

## Brigadier General Bruce Bramlette

Karl Louther was born in St. Joseph, Missouri on March 27, 1901. His family moved to Fort Benton where he graduated from high school in 1917. He attended the University of Michigan then enlisted in the Marine Corps in October 1925. Louther was commissioned in 1928, and saw duty aboard the battleships *USS Mississippi* and *USS Colorado*. As a Captain, he joined the famed Fourth Marine Division in Shanghai in 1937 and was present when the Japanese attacked China. In 1941 he became a special messenger in the Pacific Theater. In November 1944 Captain Louther was assigned to the Sixth Marine Division, was promoted to colonel and fought with the division on Okinawa. After the war he was reassigned to China before the occupation. Colonel Louther was Commandant of the Marine Barracks at Norfolk, Virginia for four years. He retired from the Corps as a Brigadier General on May 31, 1956.

The last of Fort Benton's Flag officers, Bruce Bramlette served during the Cold War era after World War II. He was born on April 20, 1940 and graduated from Fort Benton High School in 1958. Bramlette was commissioned and joined the Montana Air National Guard after graduation from Montana State University. He served in the 120th Fighter Squadron from 1962 to 1969 when he received his wings. Bramlette was a pilot in the 186th Fighter Interceptor Squadron from 1969 to 1974 and served as Executive Officer and Base Air Operations Officer. In 1975 he was Section Commander for the 120th Combat Support Squadron, and was a pilot with the William Tell team that won first place in world-wide Air Force competition for fighter squadrons in 1976. Bramlette was Chief of Supply for the 120th from 1980 to 1987 and in 1988 he became Squadron Commander. He was promoted to Brigadier General on August 12, 1992 and named Assis-

tant Adjutant General for Air Headquarters Montana National Guard. General Bramlette retired from the Air Force in 1995.

## Historic Preservation and Restoration

Prior to the nation's Bicentennial, important events occurred that helped preserve Fort Benton's history. The biggest single turning point was in 1973 when Congress passed an act designating 150

miles downriver from Fort Benton as a National Wild and Scenic River, halting any further dam construction. Fort Bentonites are grateful to Montana's U.S. Senator Lee Metcalfe for his untiring work and to the National Park Service who unfortunately lost out as the management agency. The river, its Lewis and Clark legacy and its importance as a national waterway were saved for posterity. Danger to its beauty and conservation of its resources are still a concern. Haphazard river management, disregard by landowners, and too little funding from the Federal government need to be addressed to assure the river's proper care.

*Left:* *St. Paul's Episcopal Church, completed in 1880, received major restoration in 1975. It is the oldest Episcopal Church in Montana.*

In 1975 Dorothy McLeish willed her home to the Community Improvement Association. The adobe house was built by I.G. Baker in 1866 for his wife, and was where Governor Meagher ate his last meal. The structure has been restored for public viewing. One of the two rooms is of the 1860-1870 era with whitewashed adobe walls and period bedroom furniture. The second room was remodeled into the late 1870's and early 1880's vintage with new roof line and clapboard siding. Wallpaper and a marble fireplace are appropriate to the living room setting. On display is I.G. Baker's piano brought upriver for his wife. She stayed in Fort Benton only one year, and refused to ever return!

St. Paul's Episcopal Church underwent major restoration in 1975, including re-leading its beautiful stained glass windows. The church is open to the public and conducts regular services. It is the oldest Episcopal Church in Montana and the oldest church in Fort Benton. Some renovation of Fort Benton's Engine House oc-

curred in 1976 to house its restored 1881 pumper. It is also open to the public.

The Civil War three-inch rifle probably came to Fort Benton after the Spanish-American War, but could have come with the military in 1869. Sister cannons are located at Gettysburg and Antietam. This restoration and improvements at the Museum of the Upper Missouri were accomplished by Ray Bennett.

When there was talk of building a new courthouse, County Commissioner Pierre Peres cham-

*Below: 1864 Civil War three-inch rifle may have came to Fort Benton with the military in 1869.*

*Right: I.G. Baker store and warehouse were destroyed after the building was condemned in 1975.*

pioned exterior restoration of the original 1884 building. His action saved one of Fort Benton's most beautiful Victorian structures from the fate of the old 1881 jail that was razed for a parking lot.

In 1975 the abandoned I.G. Baker Co. store and warehouse, built a hundred years earlier, was torn down. It had served the community well, but had fallen into such a state of

*Below: W.G. Conrad Mansion just before it was burned to make way for a parking lot*

disrepair that it had to be condemned. In its heyday the structure was the headquarters for Montana's largest mercantile business. It was also the community opera house, gymnasium and theater for Chouteau County High School, community civic center and finally a bowling alley. Its Victoriana was replaced by a ghastly architectural monstrosity courtesy of the U.S. Postal Service.

The town was unable to save two other important historic structures. The Conrad Mansion was demolished by the Catholic Church in favor of . . . a parking lot. The last two stories of the Benton Record building came crashing down to be replaced by the Community Bible Church and . . . another parking lot. For some reason, a place to park automobiles was a destructive force in the history of Fort Benton. On a more positive note, the Grand Union Hotel received its first restoration funds and work began to save the grand old lady.

**Left:** *Fort Benton's first fire engine after its restoration*

**Above:** *Old Engine House, later the City Hall, received partial restoration in 1975.*

## Montana Memorial and the Bicentennial

Four years before the National Bicentennial, Fort Benton began searching for an appropriate gift for the nation's birthday. The people at the River Press, Joel F. Overholser and his niece Joan, found a long-forgotten project that was lost during the Great Depression: the State of Montana's memorial to the Lewis and Clark Expedition.

This heroic-sized bronze statue of the Two Captains,

Sacagawea and baby Jean Baptiste by Bob Scriver was the gift of this small town to the State of Montana and to the nation, and commemorates the most important exploration done in our country's history. The project was one of only thirty cited throughout the United States as an exemplary effort, and the only project in Montana to receive such recognition.

In 1929, Fort Benton was officially designated by the State Legislature as the site for the state's memorial to Lewis and Clark. Charles M. Russell was

**Left:** *Charlie Bovey's Old Town at the fairgrounds in Great Falls displayed Jos. Sullivan's Saddlery.*

185

selected as the artist for the bronze statue, but no funding was appropriated by the state. Just in front of the old fort a circle was built in 1929 for the statue, and Russell made a preliminary sketch of the Two Captains and Sacagawea. The project died with the death of Russell and the Depression. In later years Charlie's widow Nancy Russell commissioned Henry Lyon to create a quarter-sized bronze from Charlie's sketch; that bronze is displayed at the Montana Historical Society in Helena.

The project was revived and the 1972 Legislature reaffirmed the site in Fort Benton. Governor Tom Judge appointed a state committee of Fort Bentonites to develop the memorial. Artist Bob Scriver of Browning, Montana's premier western sculptor, created the bronze statue. Both artist and committee spent the first year in historic research before a single piece of clay was modeled. The statue is titled "Decision at the Marias," a reminder of the ten days the Expedition spent deciding which fork of the river was the true Missouri.

Funds to produce the memorial were raised by selling bronze replicas of the original. Classic Bronze in southern California produced the replica editions, and Modern Art Foundry in New York cast the heroic-sized statue. All replicas were sold prior to Dedication Day on June 13, 1976.

The gala celebration was a huge success. Over 15,000 people swelled the streets of Fort Benton as Governor Judge and the artist unveiled the Memorial. It was easily the largest attendance ever at a celebration in Fort Benton.

The bronze statue was shipped from New York on a flatbed truck. Standing twelve feet

# Bicentennial Celebration 1976
## Dedication of the State Memorial to Lewis and Clark

*Above:* Bob Scriver, premier Western sculptor and artist of the State Memorial to Lewis and Clark

*Above:* Fort Benton's Bicentennial gift to the Nation

*Below:* Bicentennial Parade coming down Front Street; it was a three-hour extravaganza!

*Left:* Timberjack Joe and Tuffy, celebrities from Wyoming

*Above:* State Bicentennial Chairman Hal Stearns presenting Chairman John G. Lepley with the National Award, one of only thirty presented in the U.S.

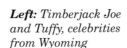

*Above:* Unveiling the statue during its dedication

*Below:* Musical Ride of the Mounted Police from Fort Macleod, Alberta

*Below:* Guest performers included headliners Jody Miller and the Hager Brothers

*Right:* Joel F. Overholser, Fort Benton's historian and the one most responsible for saving the history of the Upper Missouri and Northern Great Plains

tall, it encountered some problems with overpasses on its way to Montana! Thanks to the U.S. military, the job of moving the statue onto its base was effortless. Every commercial company had turned down the job as being too risky. With a crane, a sergeant and his crew from Malmstrom Air Force Base lifted it like a baby onto the granite rock and the Memorial was complete. Donated by Tanner Brothers, the granite base came from the Square Butte Quarry, which was also the source of Charlie Russell's tombstone. The base weighs twenty tons and elevates the statue another six feet.  Half of the stone is buried under the concrete.

The dedication occurred one hundred and seventy-one years to the day that the Expedition passed the site of Fort Benton. The entire half-million dollars raised for the project was from private sources.

No state or federal funds were involved, a real gift from the Birthplace of Montana to the Nation.

Since the 1976 Bicentennial, Fort Benton has continued to progress, grow, have gigantic celebrations, build museums, reconstruct the fort and save her history. The story of her last twenty-five years is left for another to tell.

# 150 Years Later - Fort Benton's Most Historic Symbols

**Right:** *Old Fort Benton in 1976. The blockhouse is the last vestige of Montana's fur trade and is the state's oldest standing structure. It will be incorporated into the reconstructed replica of the Blackfoot fur post, the oldest continuous white settlement in Montana.*

**Below:** *Grand Union Hotel in 1946 on Fort Benton's 100th Birthday; by 2000, the grand old lady will be ready to serve guests for another millennium.*

# Fort Benton Index

Volunteer Fire Department  93

W

Y